Horses Coloring Book For Adults

This book belongs to:

_____

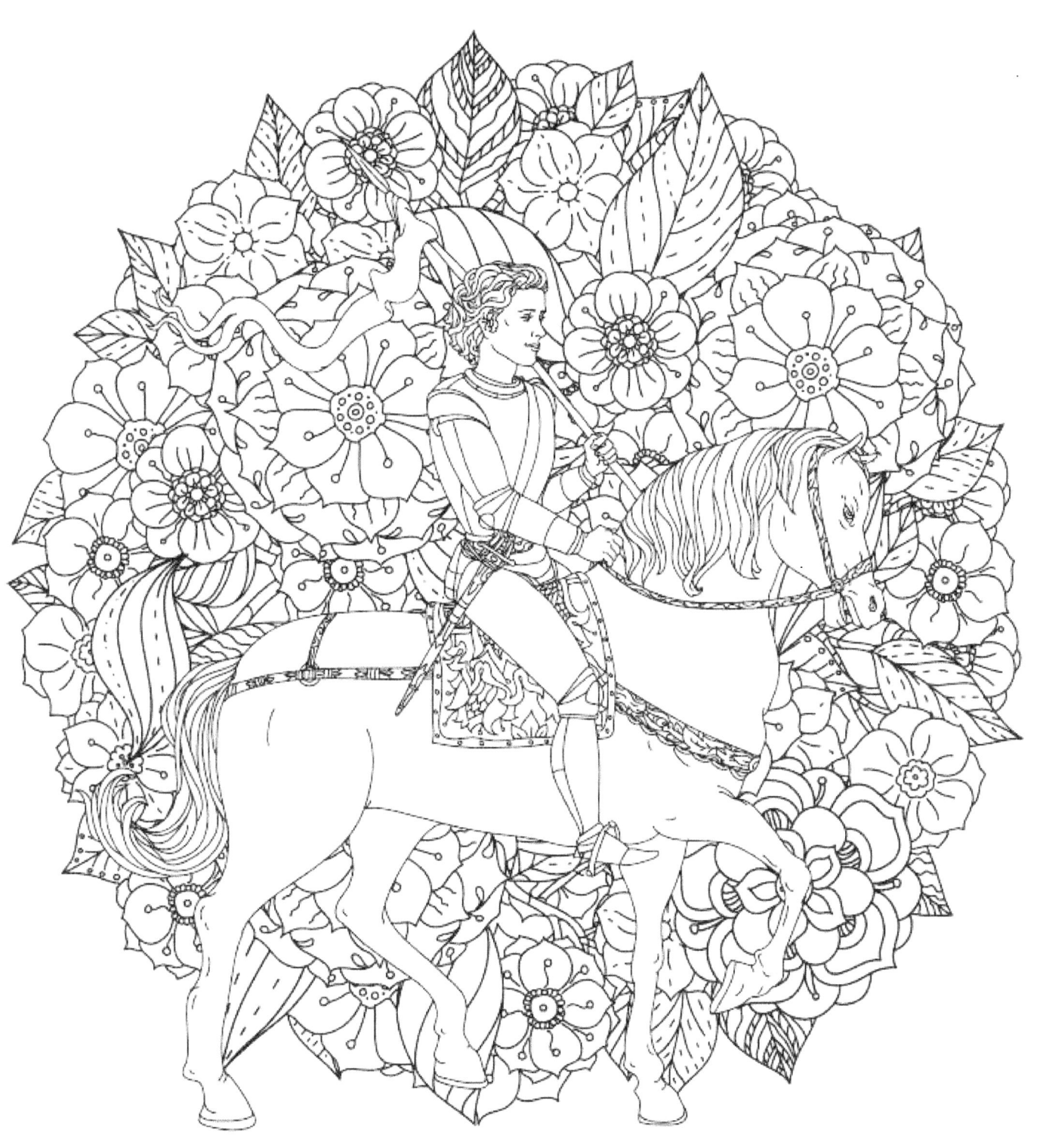

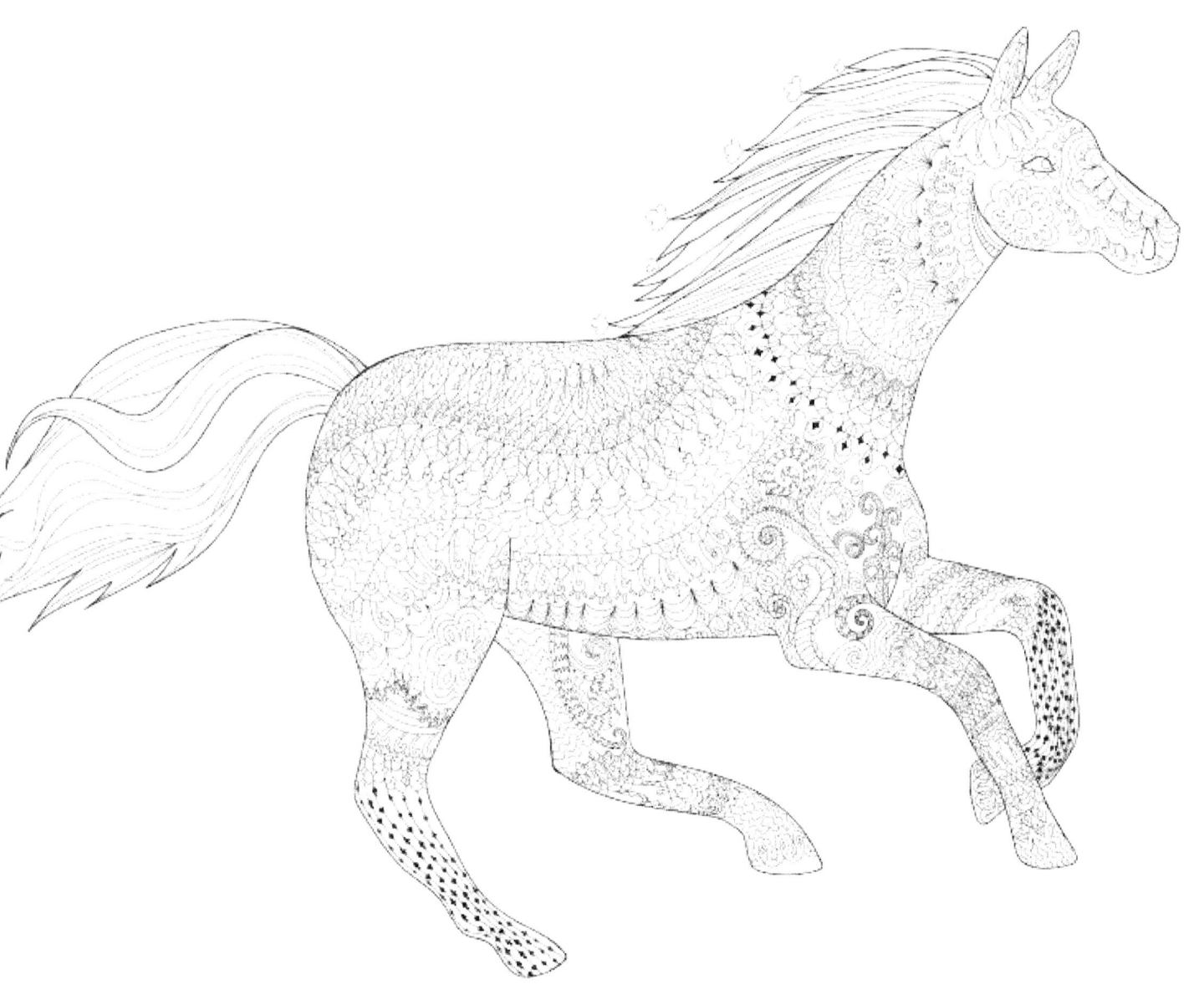

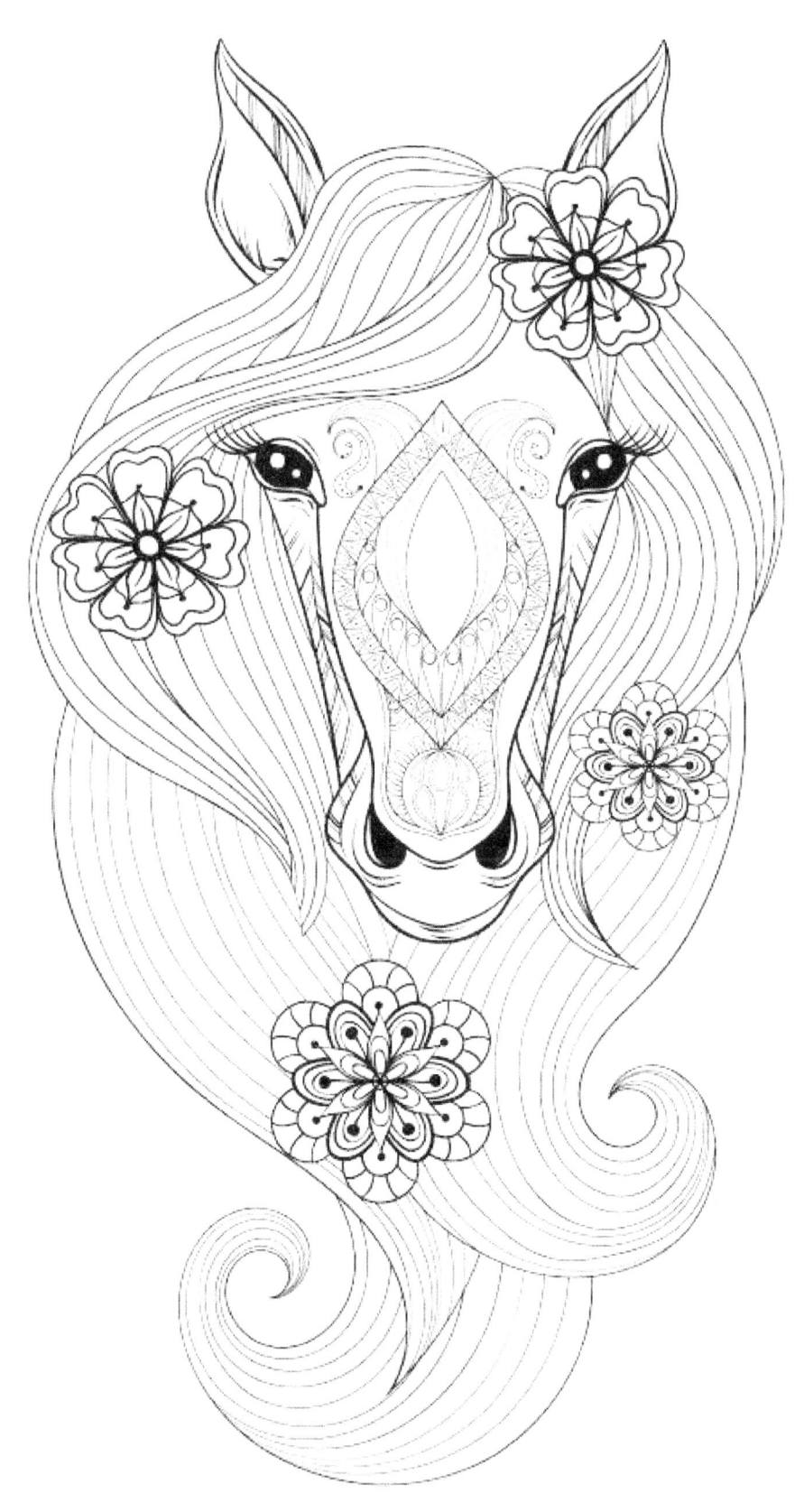

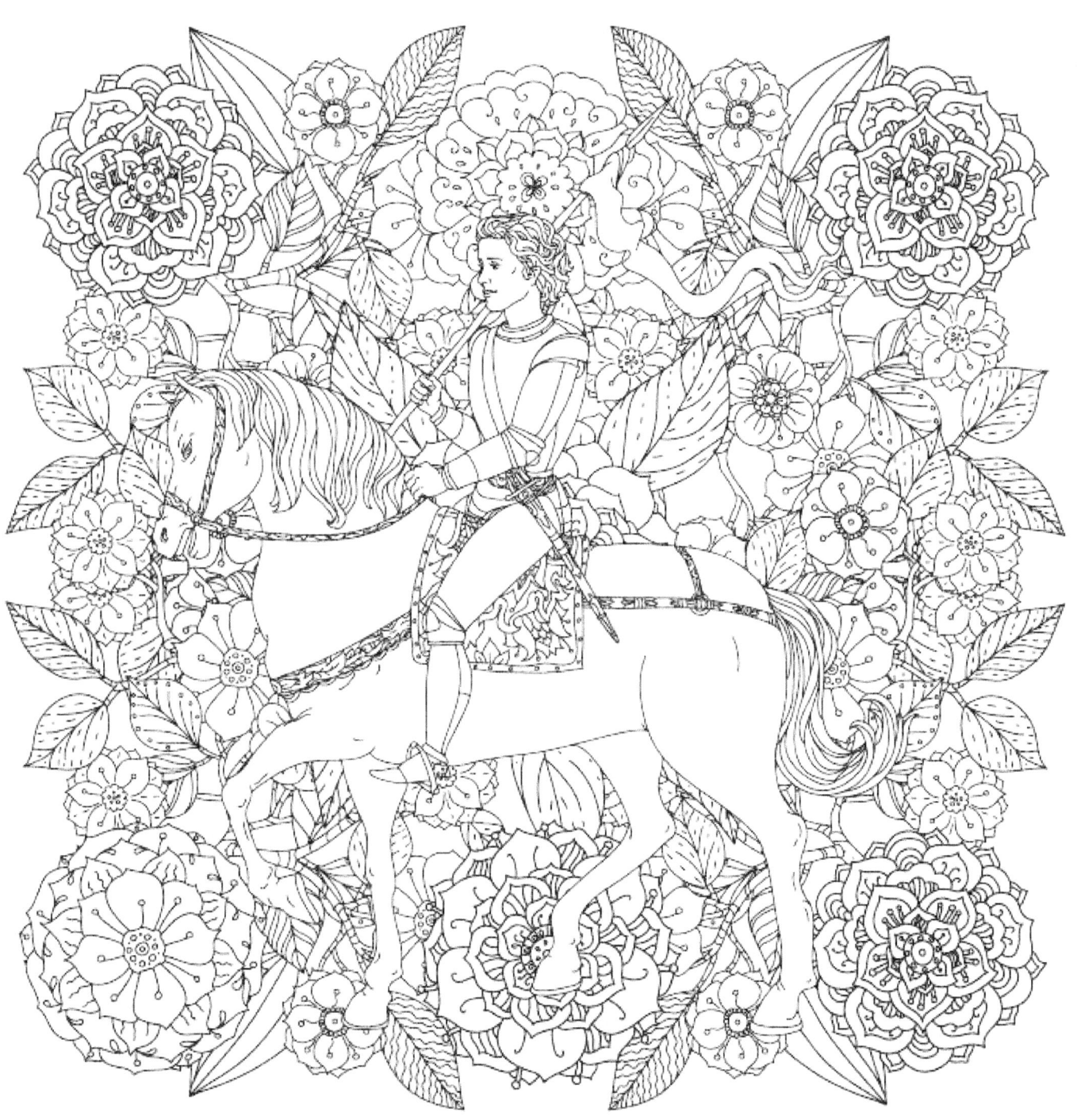

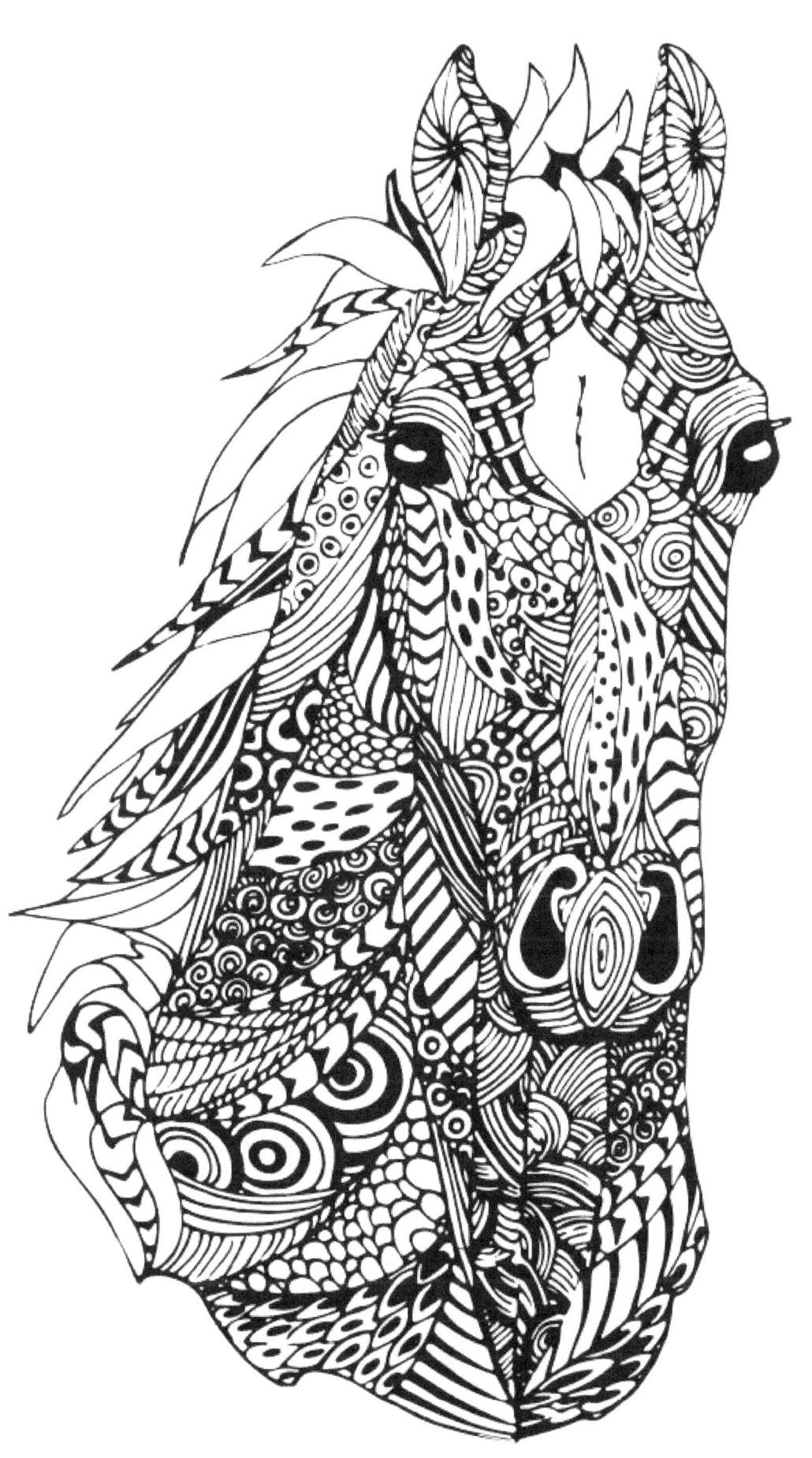

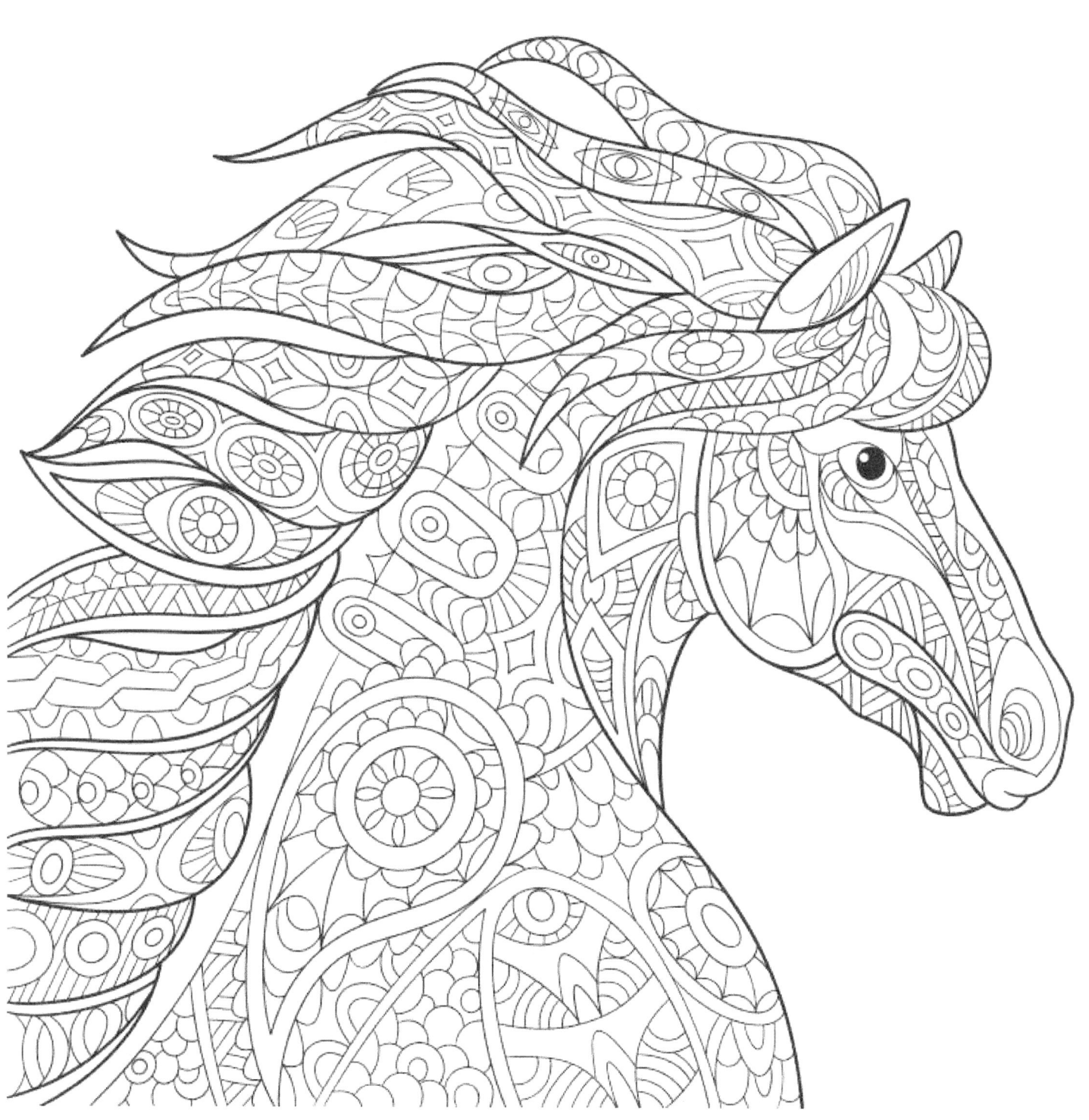

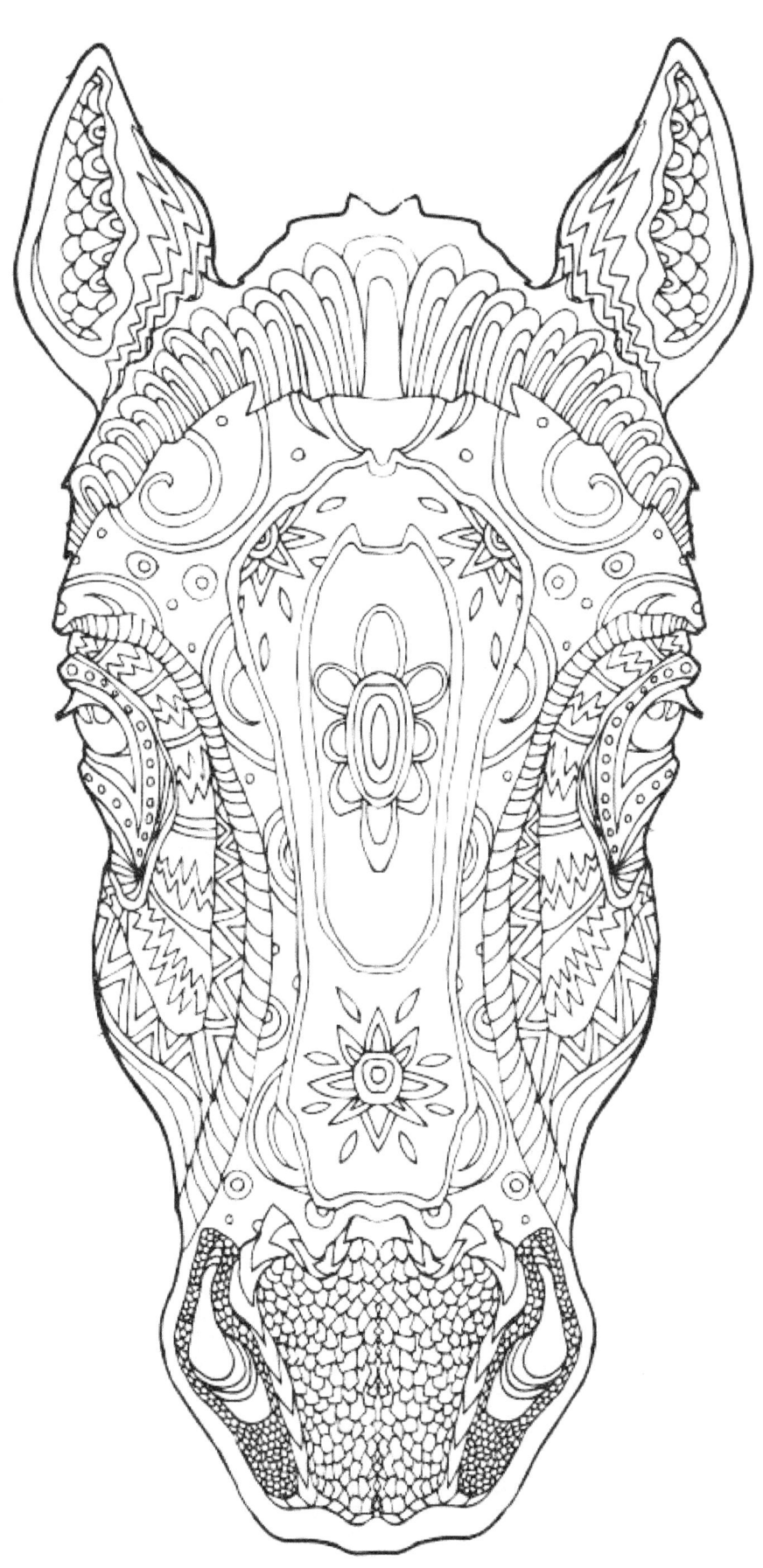

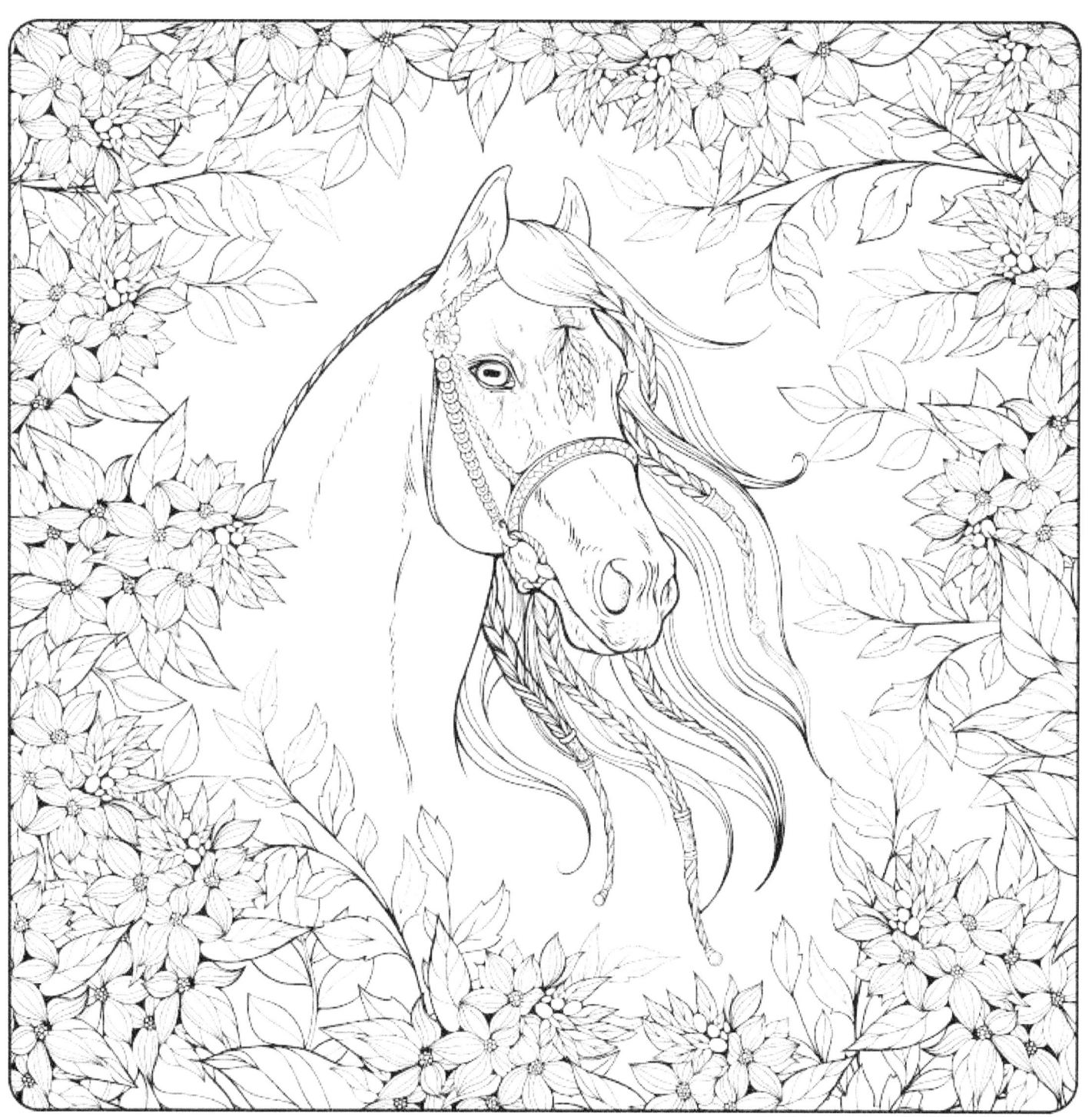

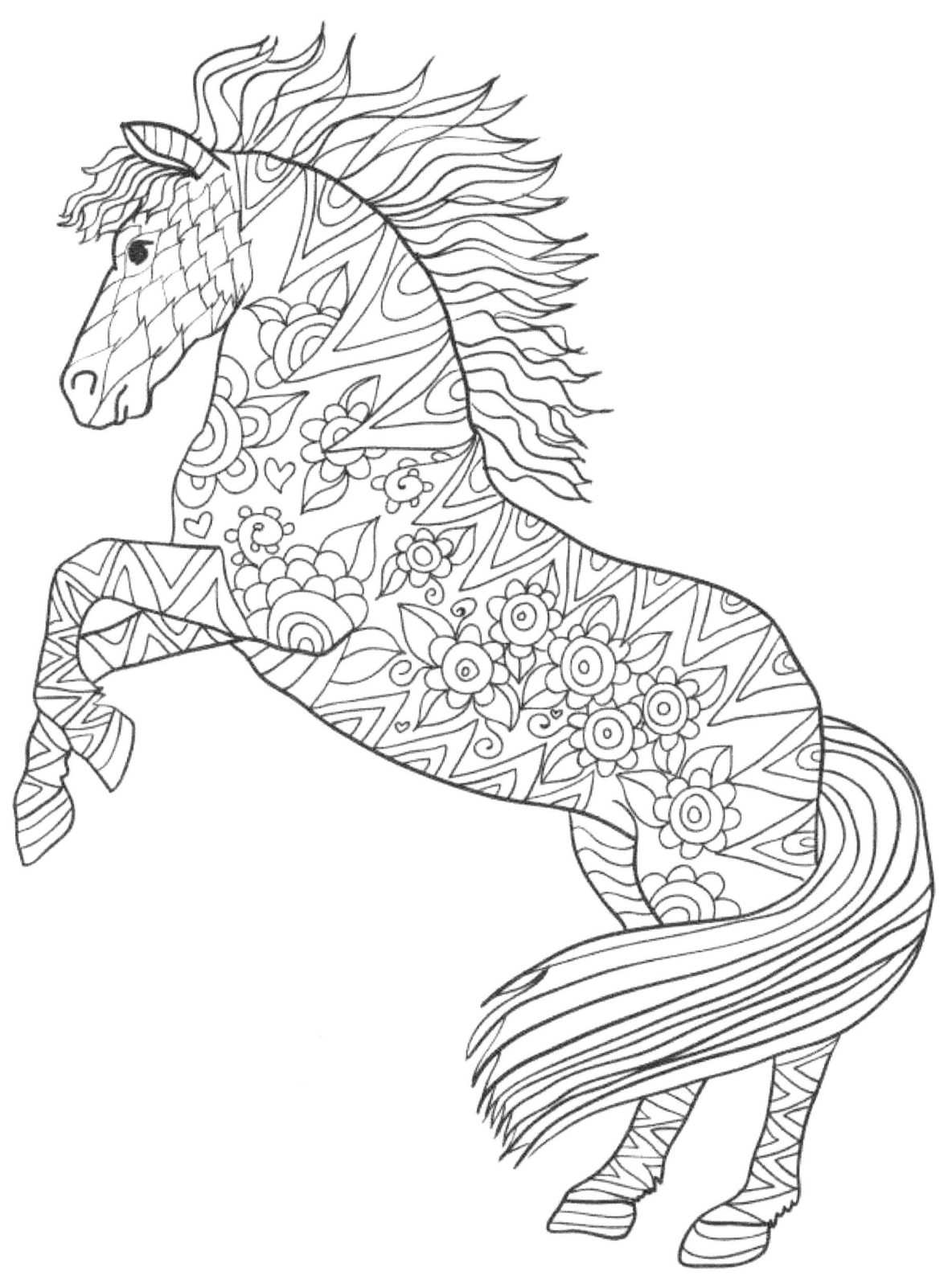

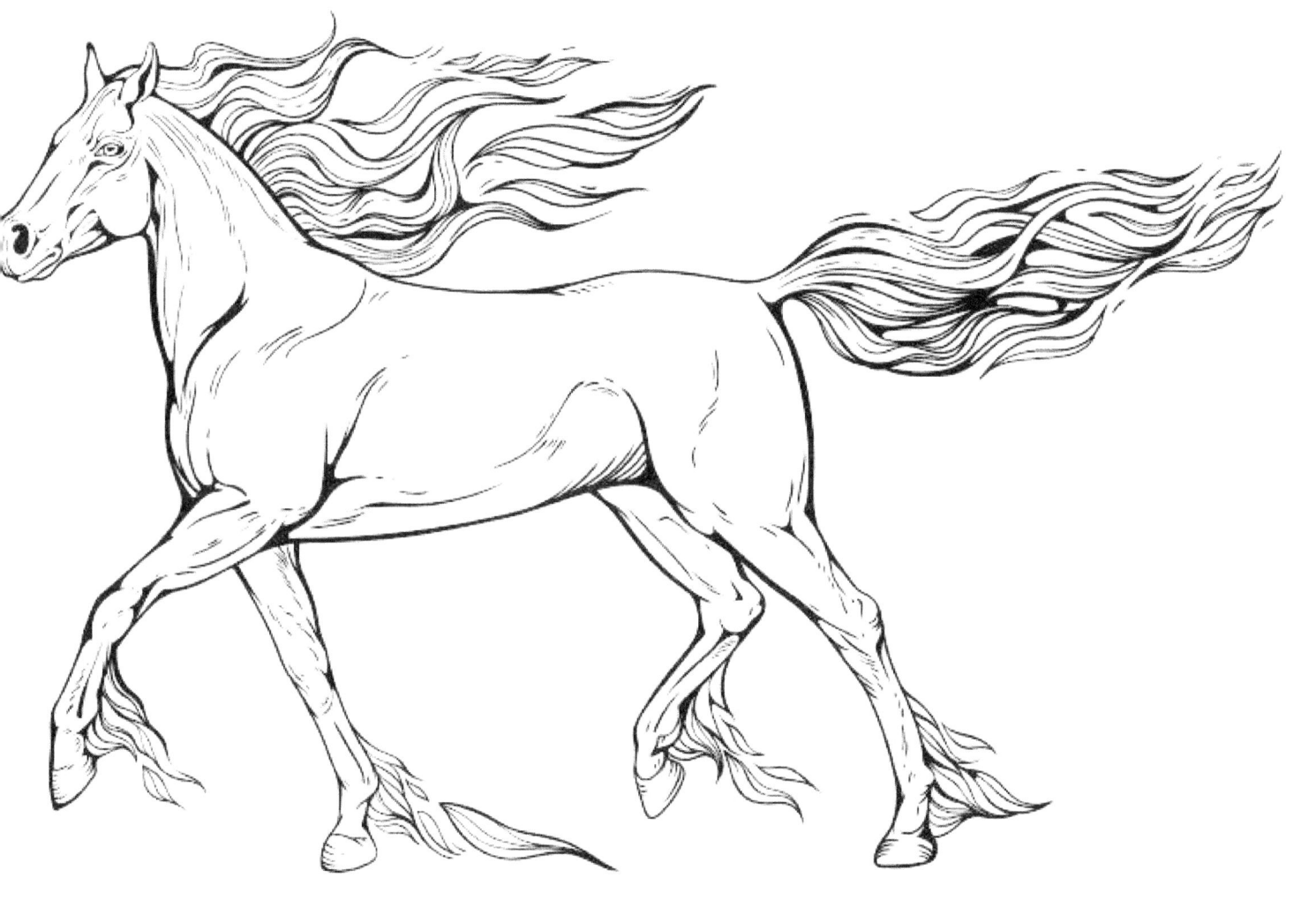

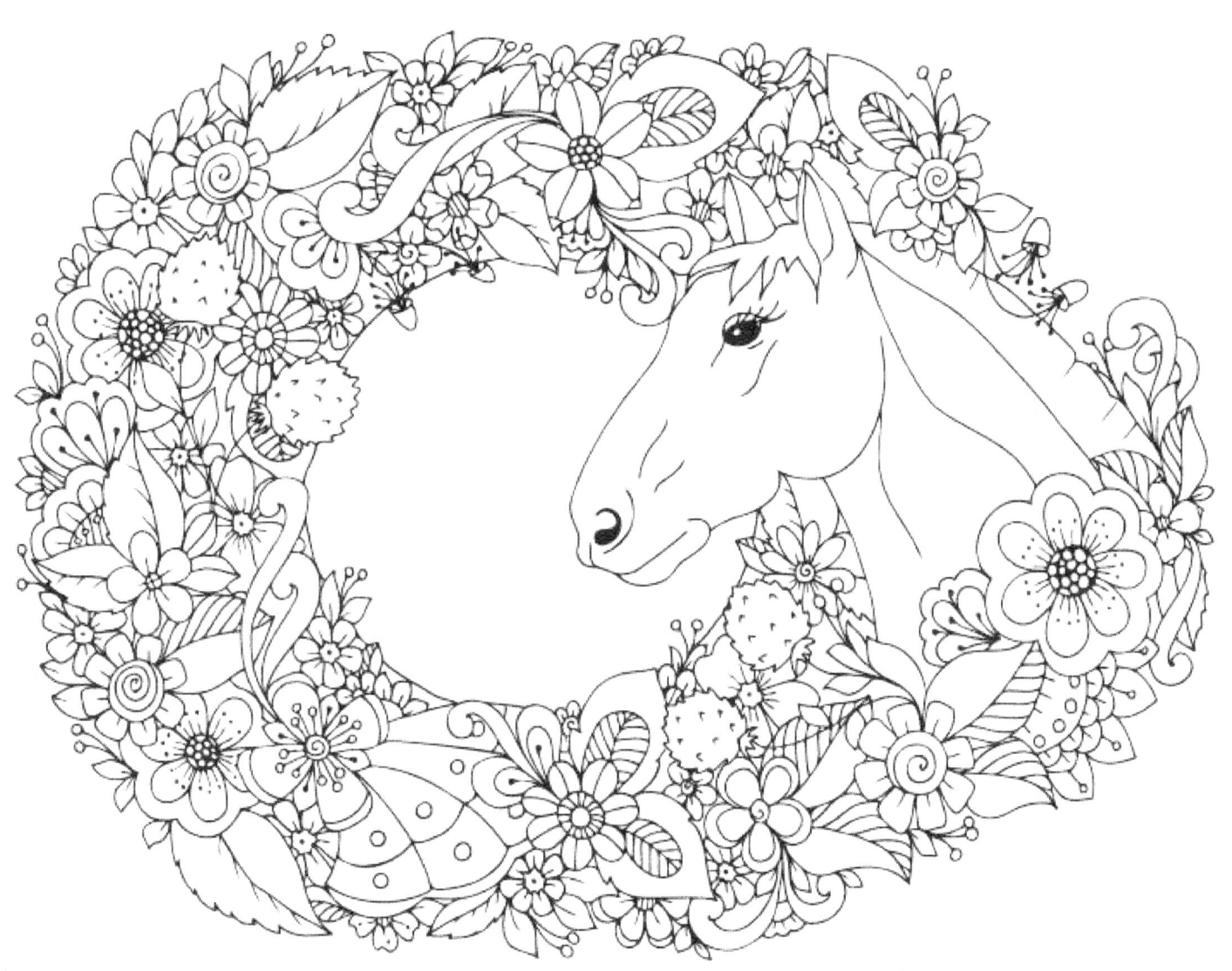

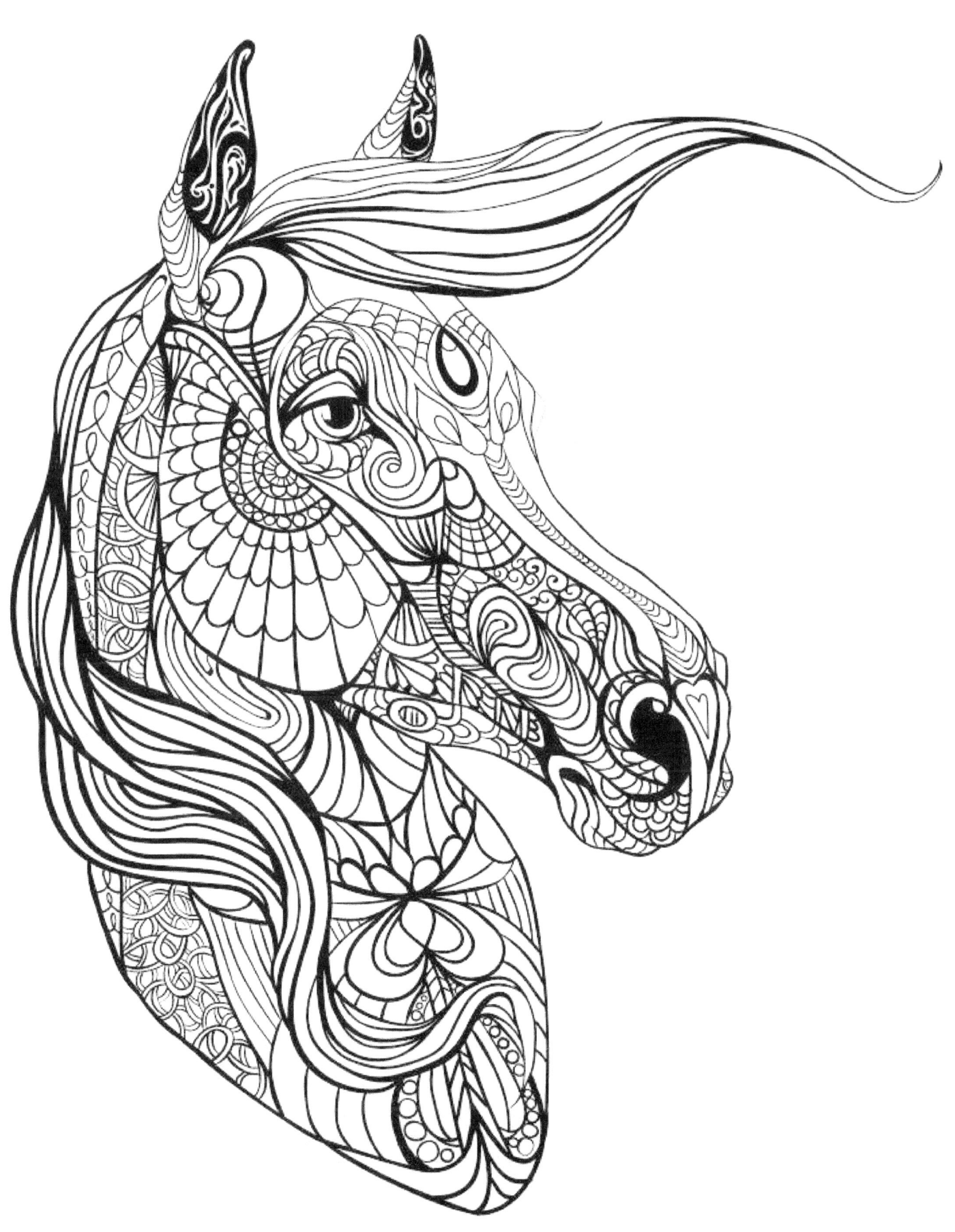

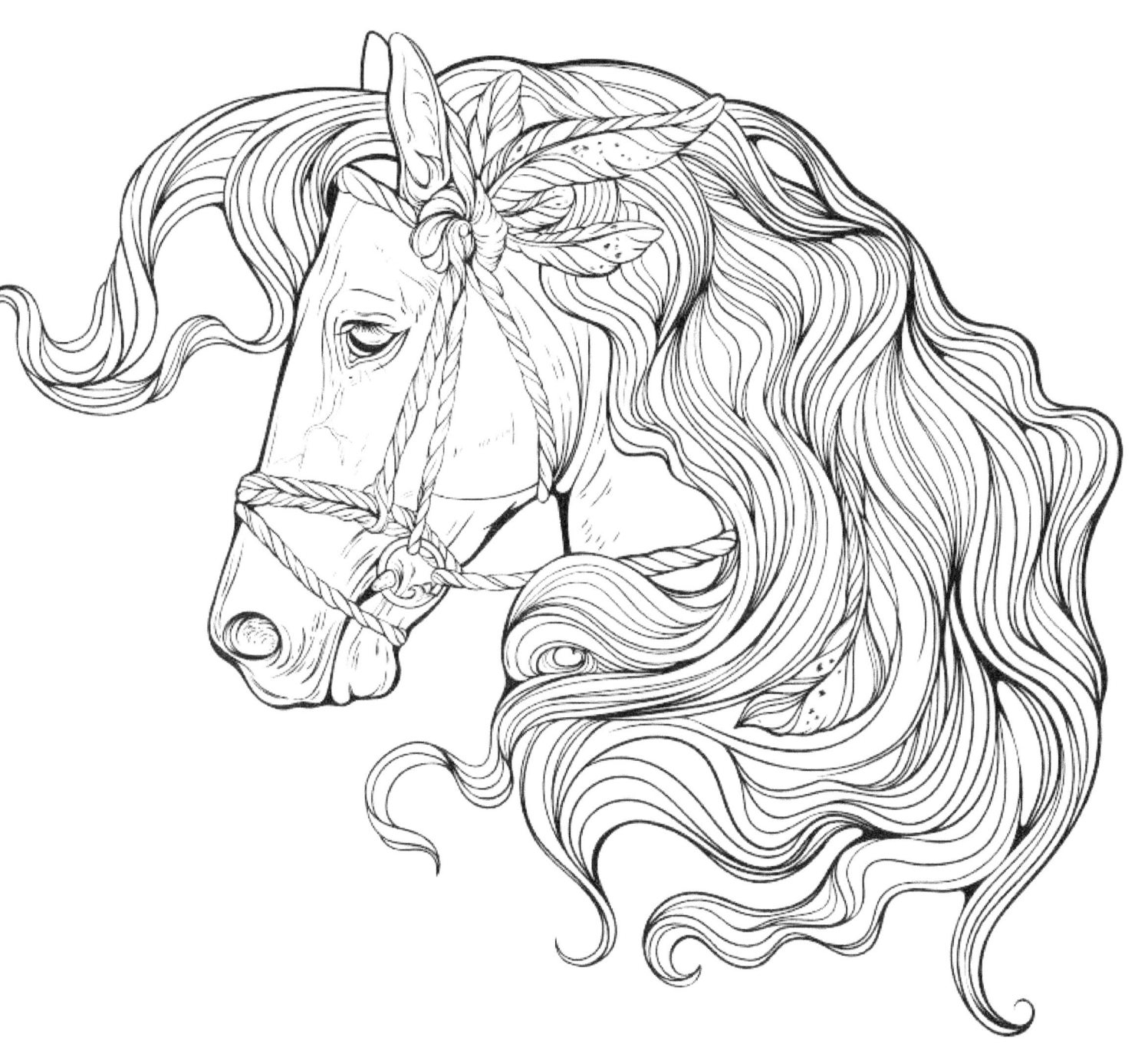

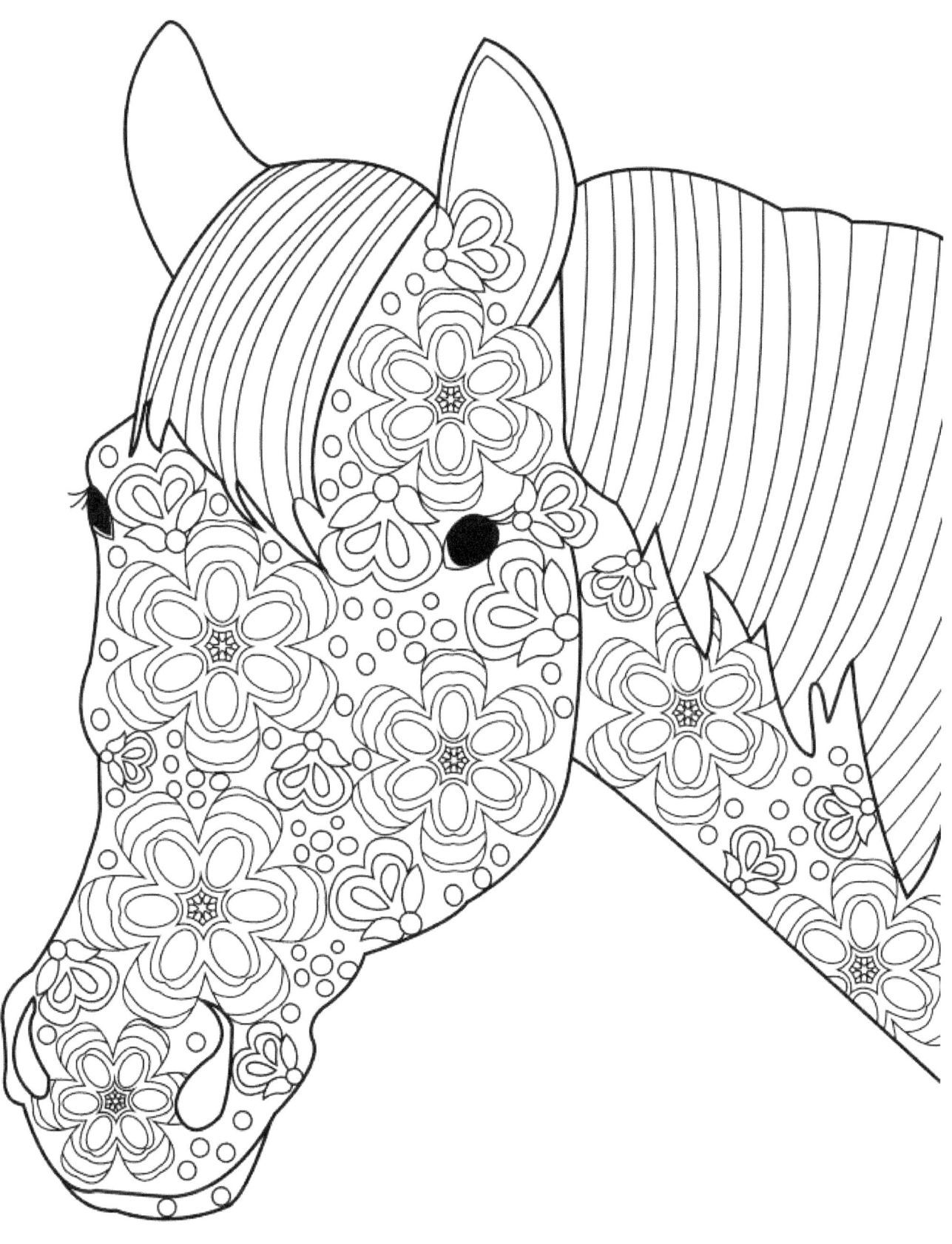

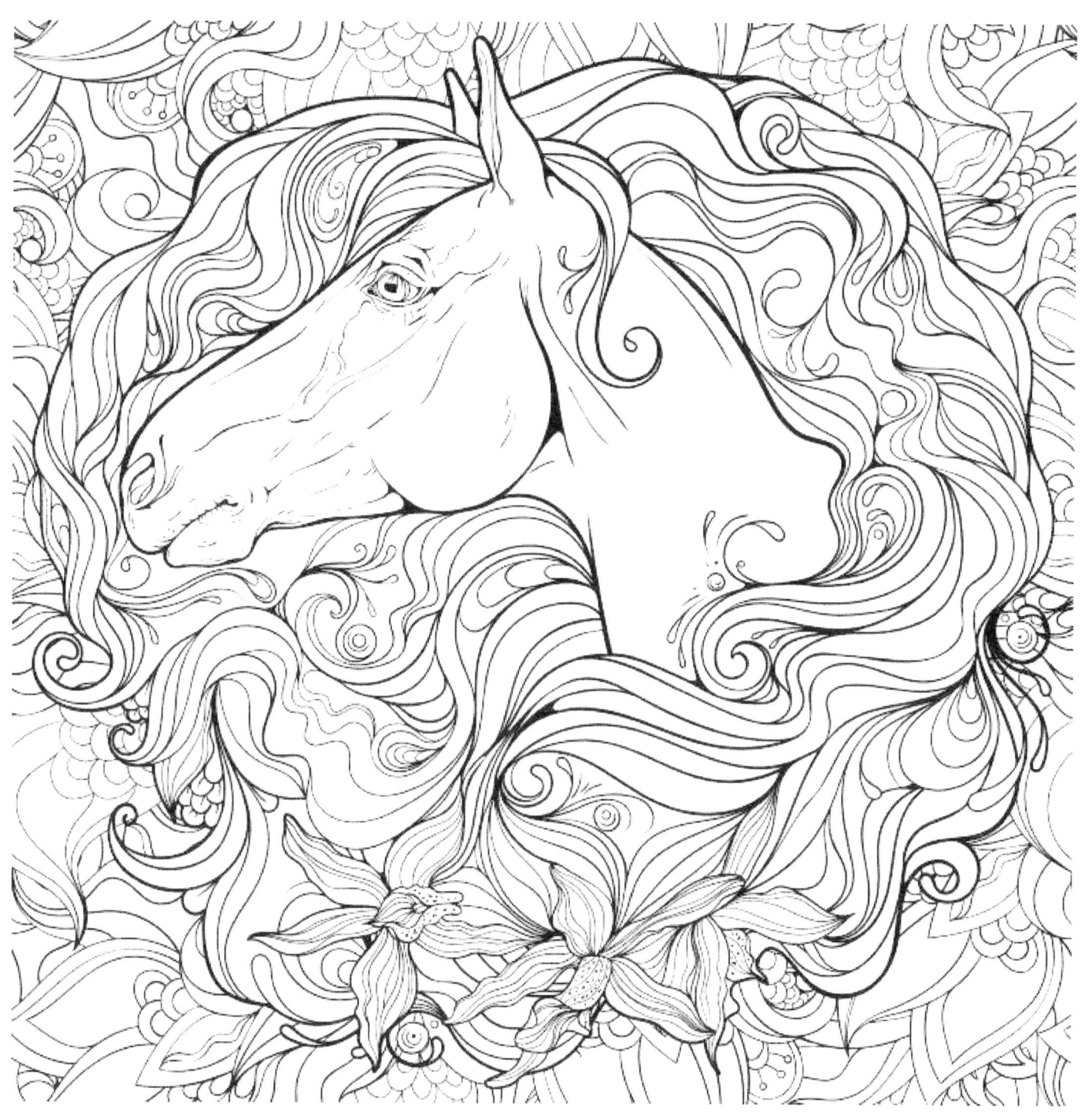

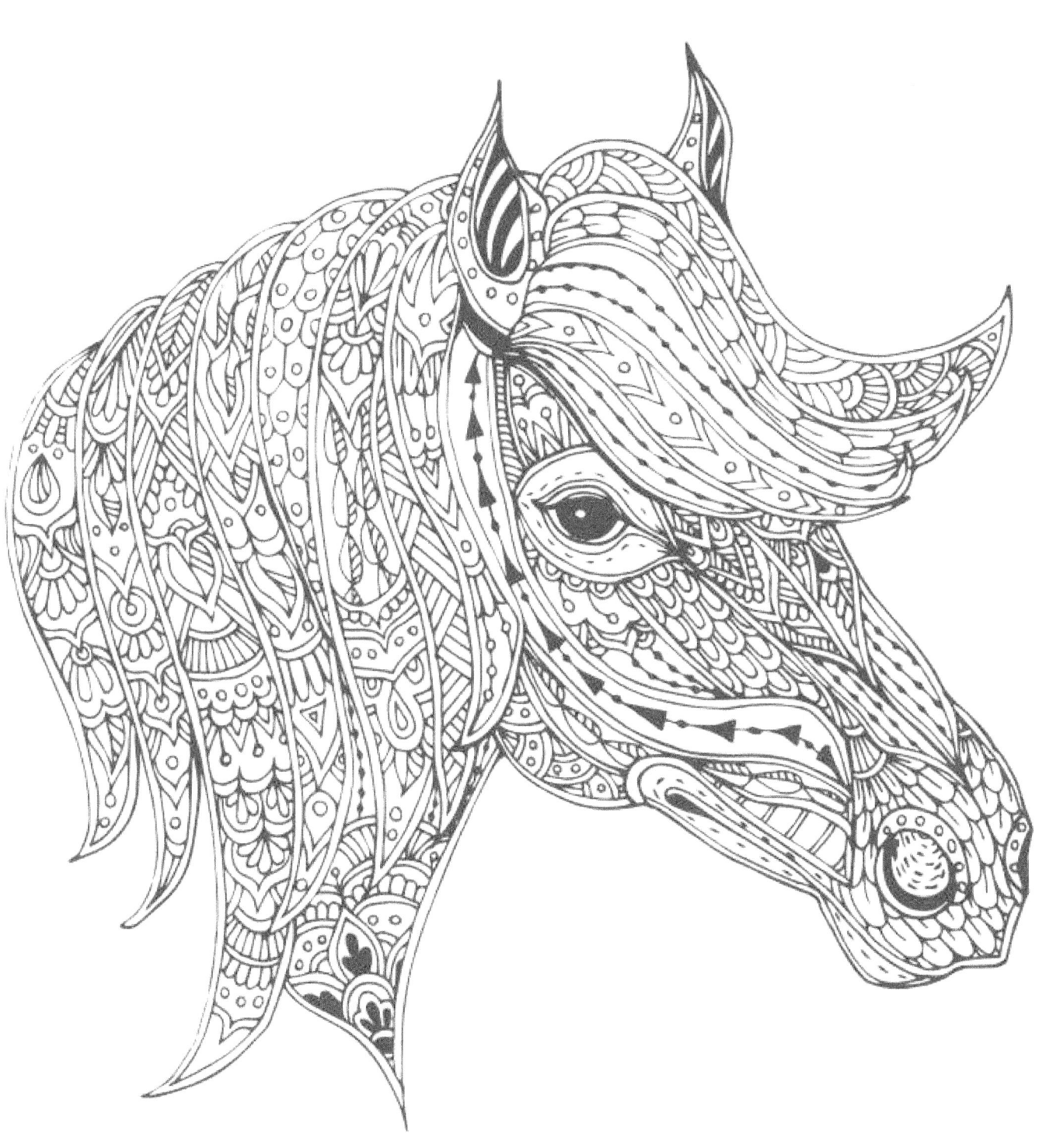

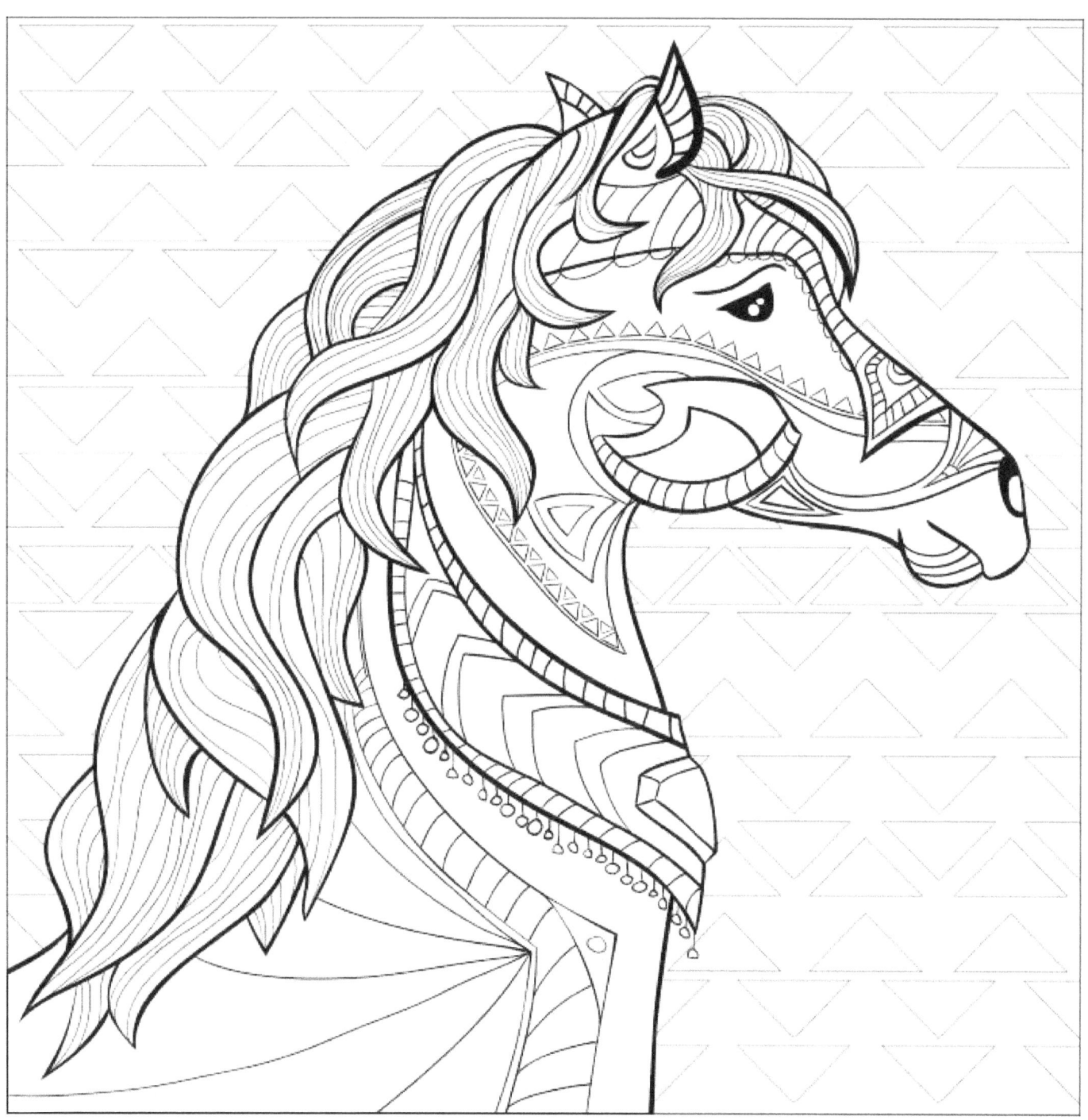

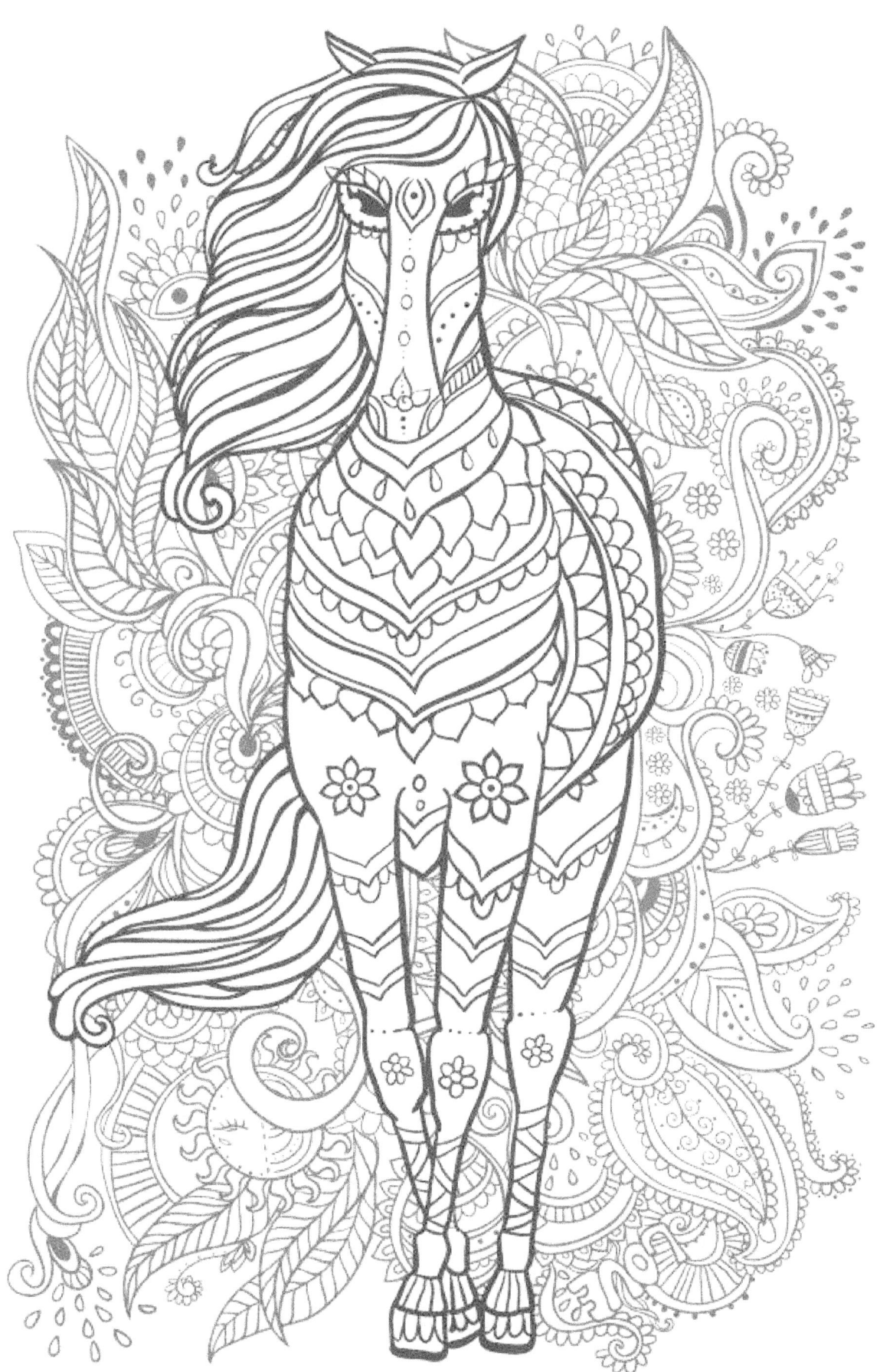

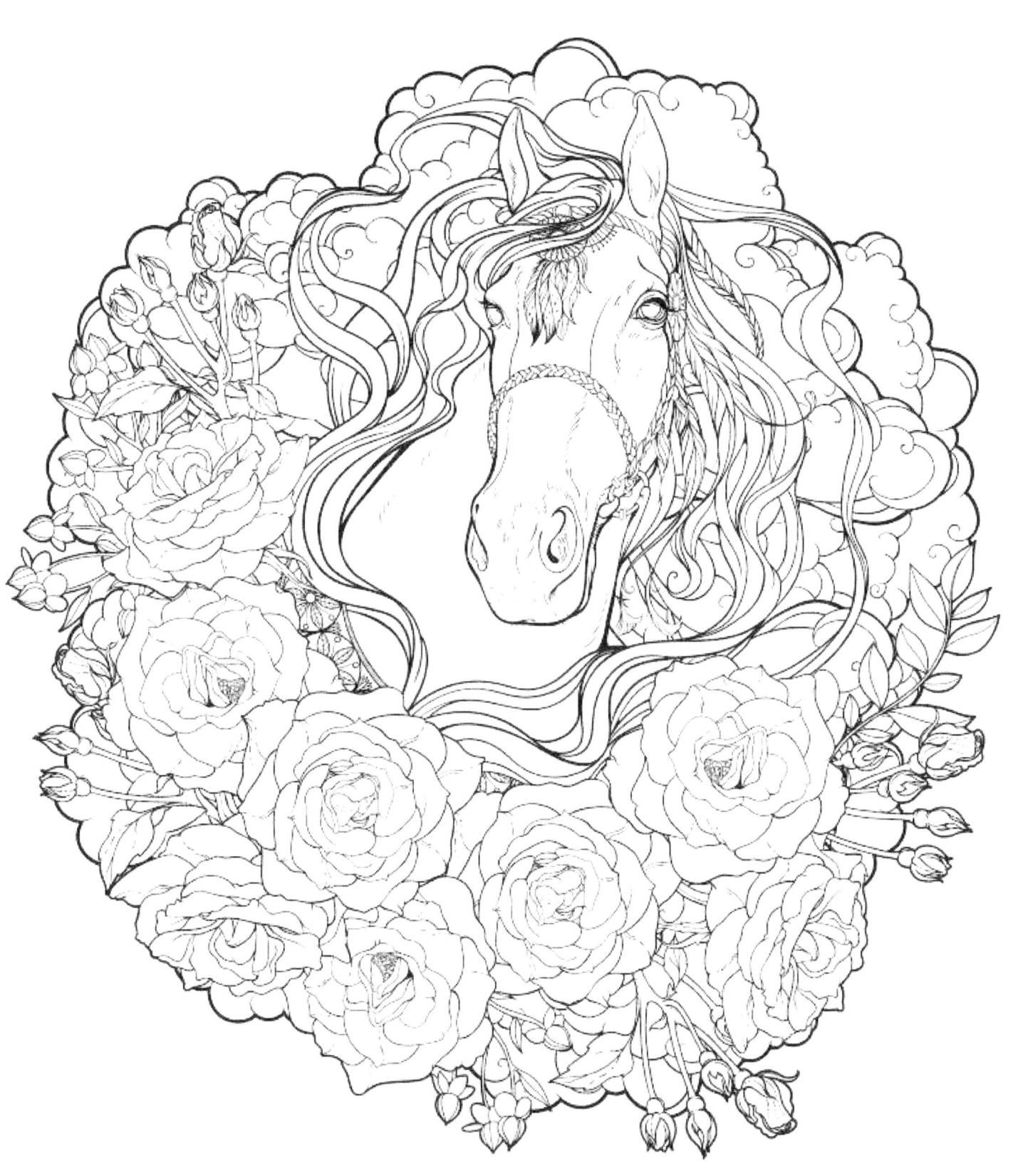

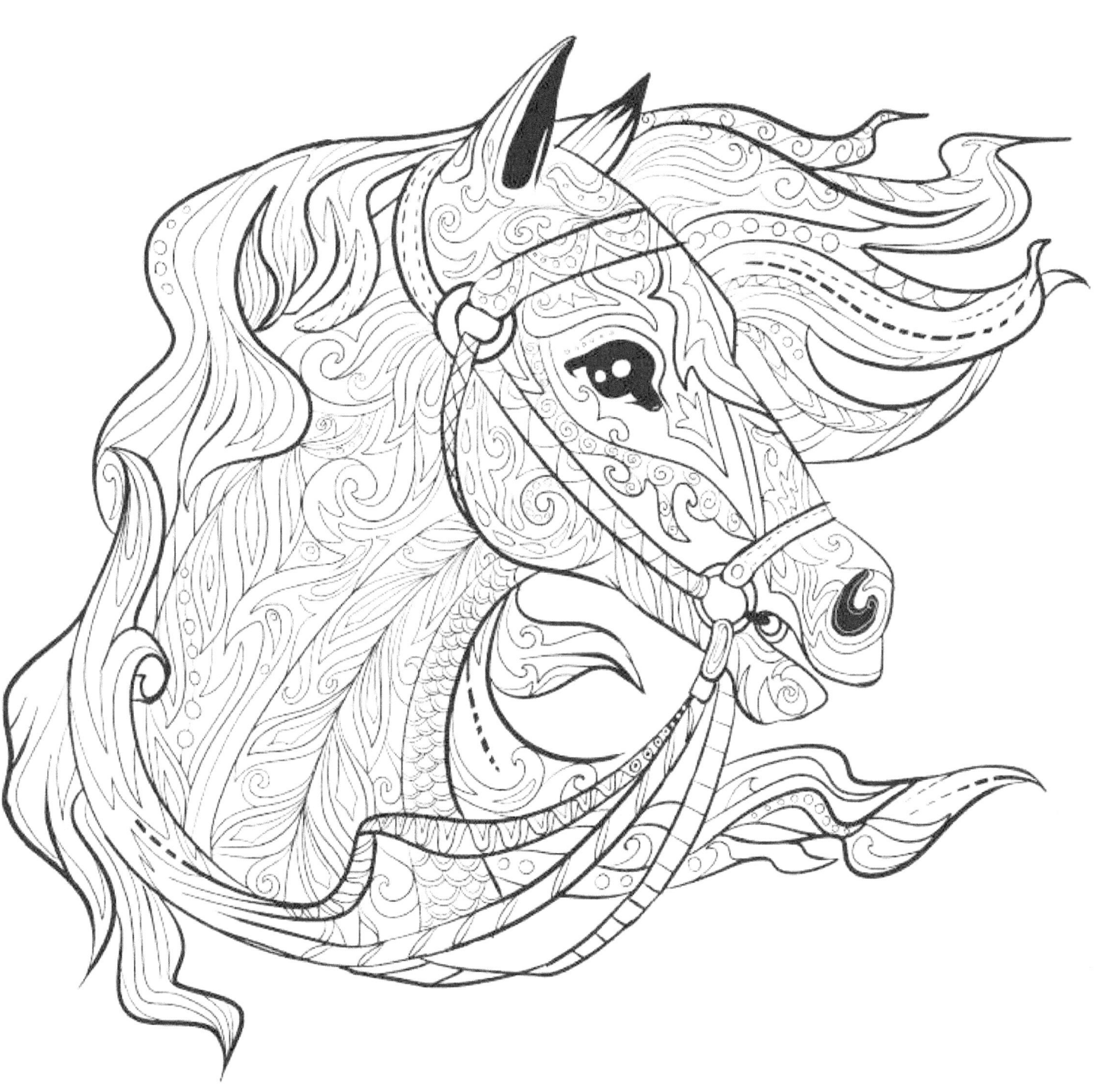

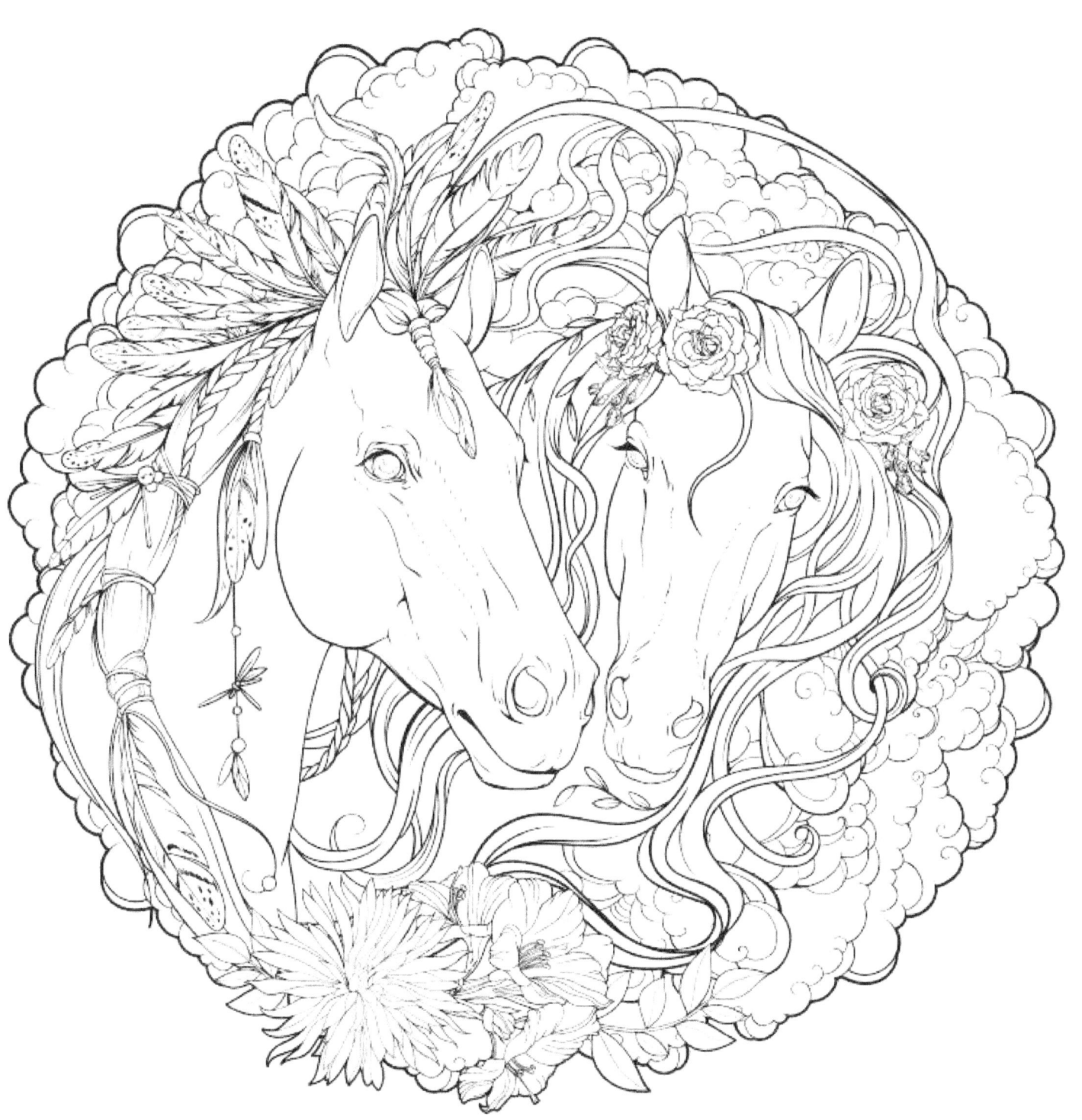

Bonus Hedgehogs and Turtles Coloring Pages to Enjoy!

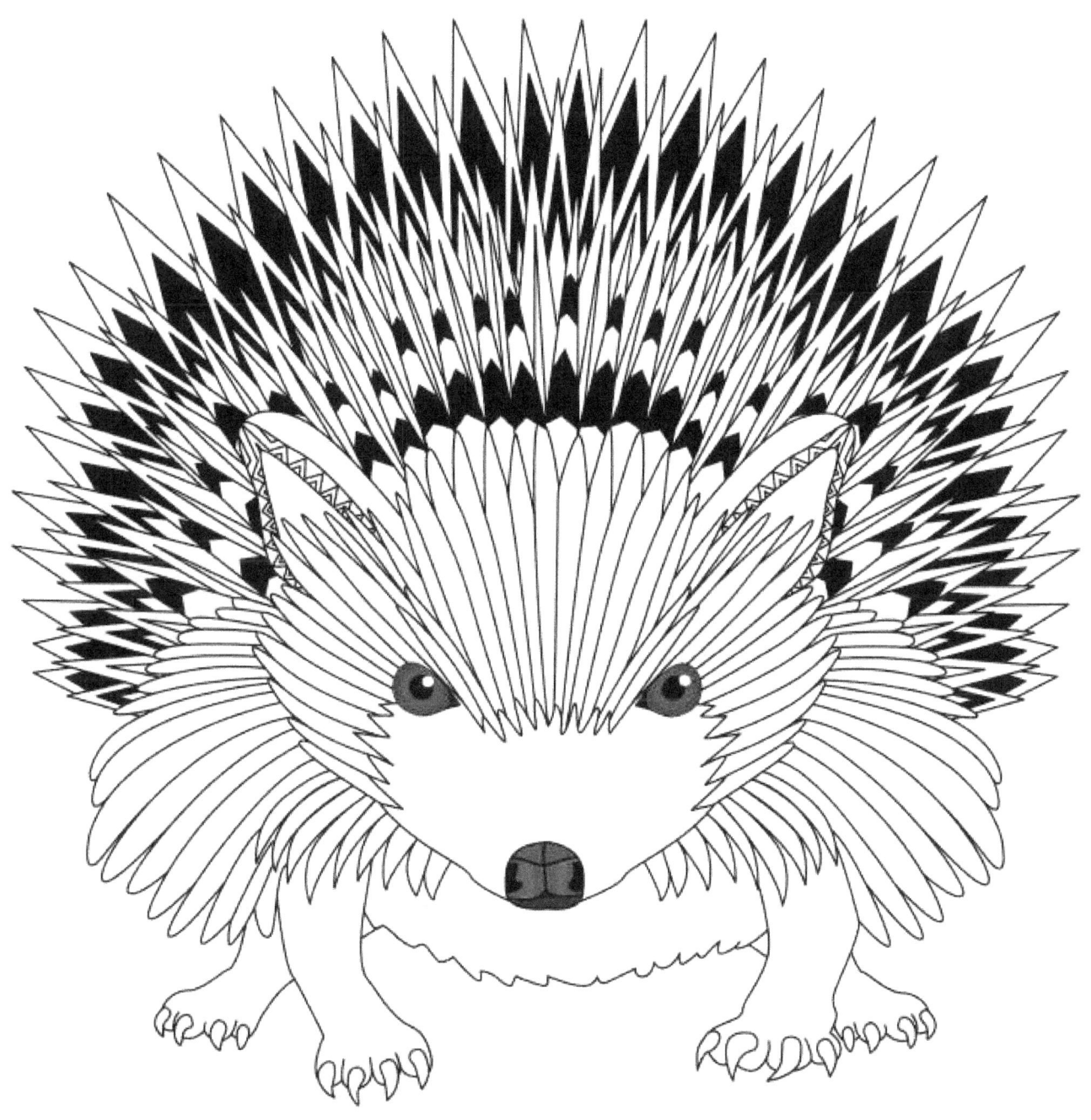

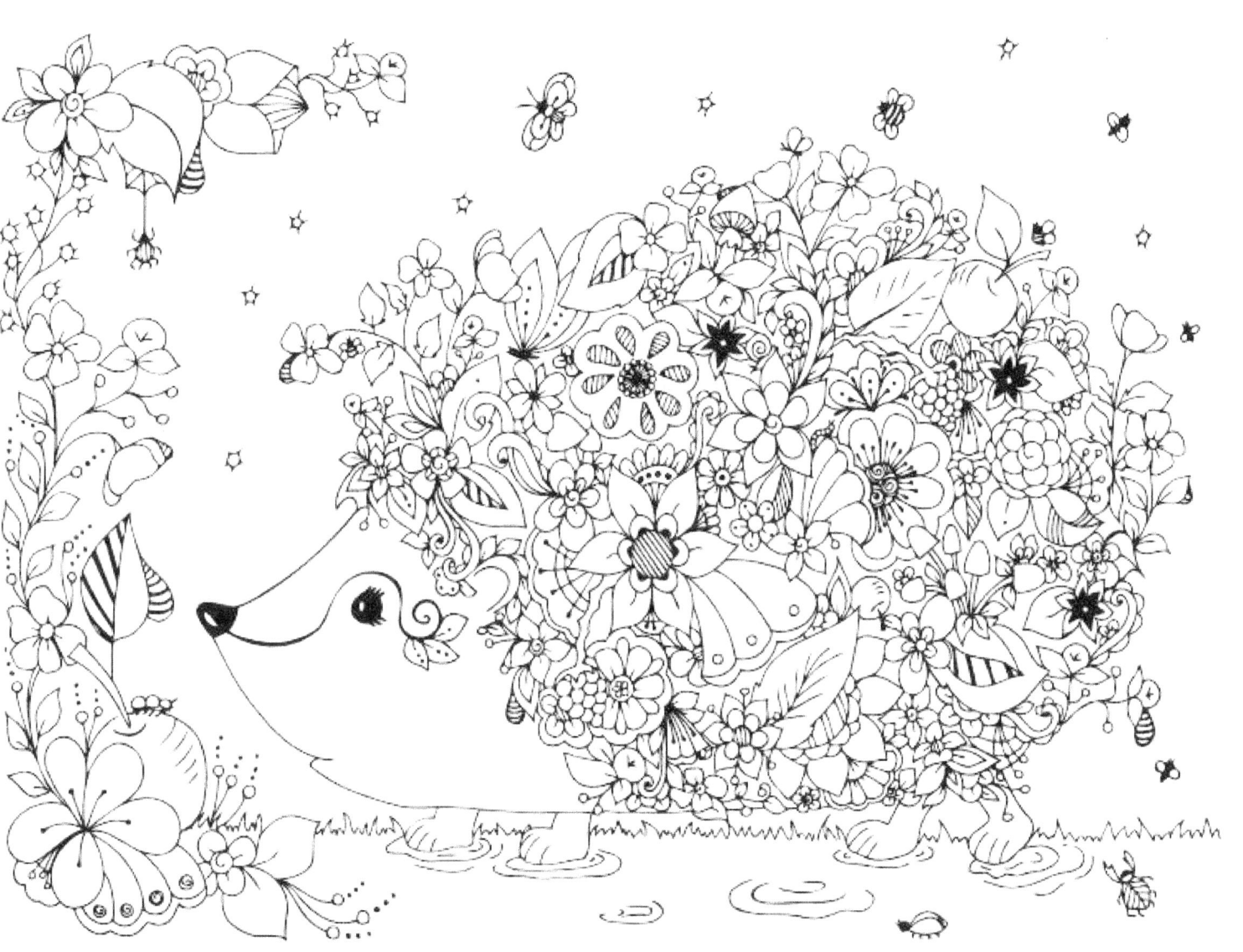

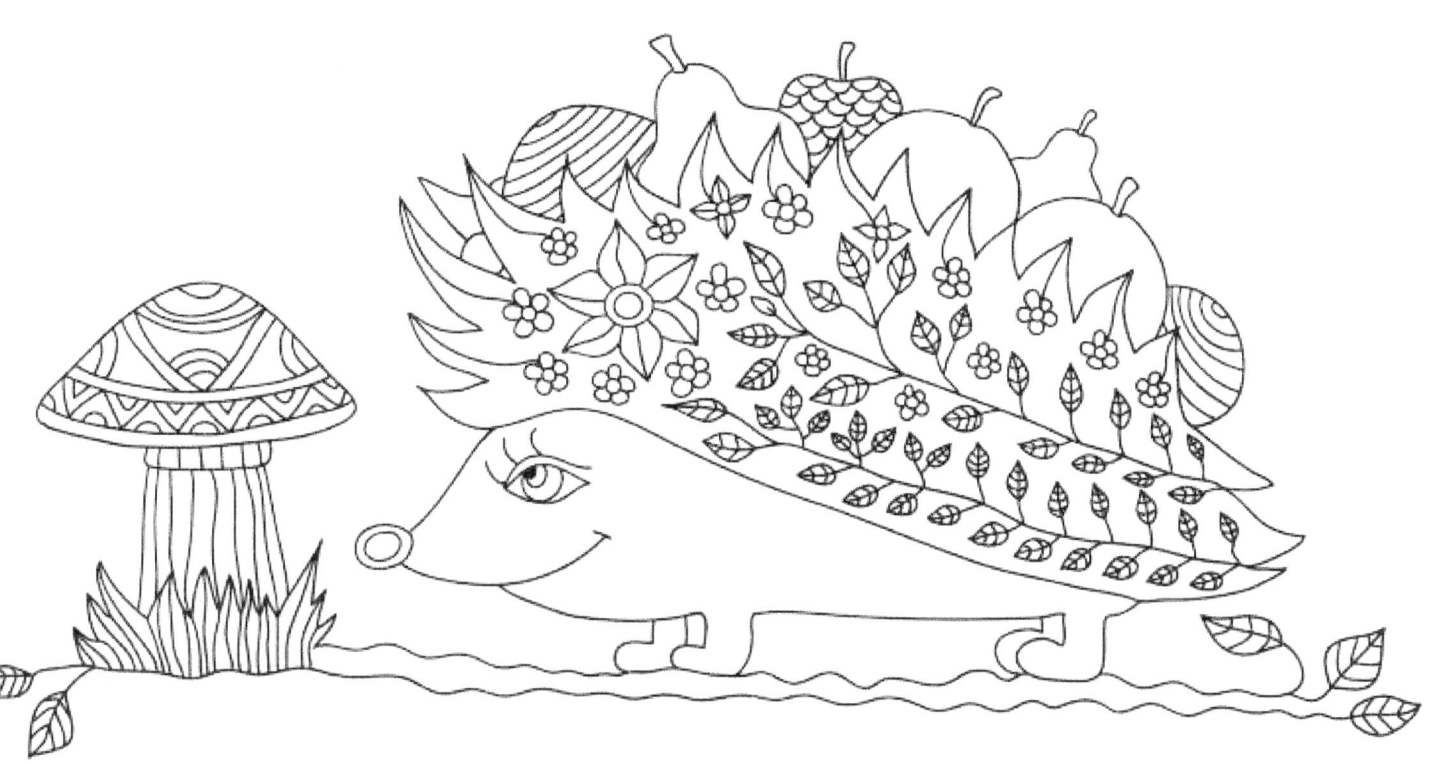

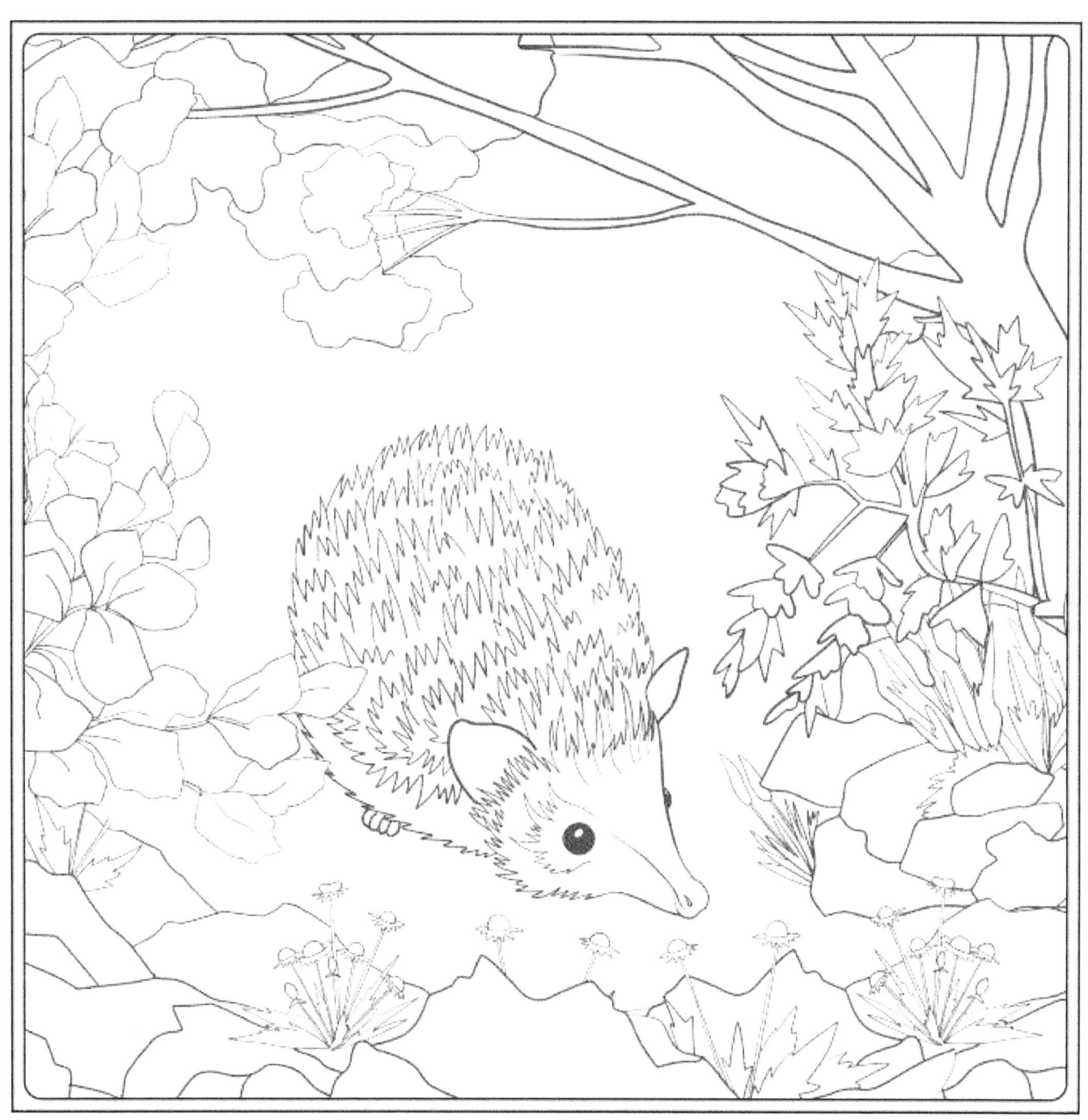

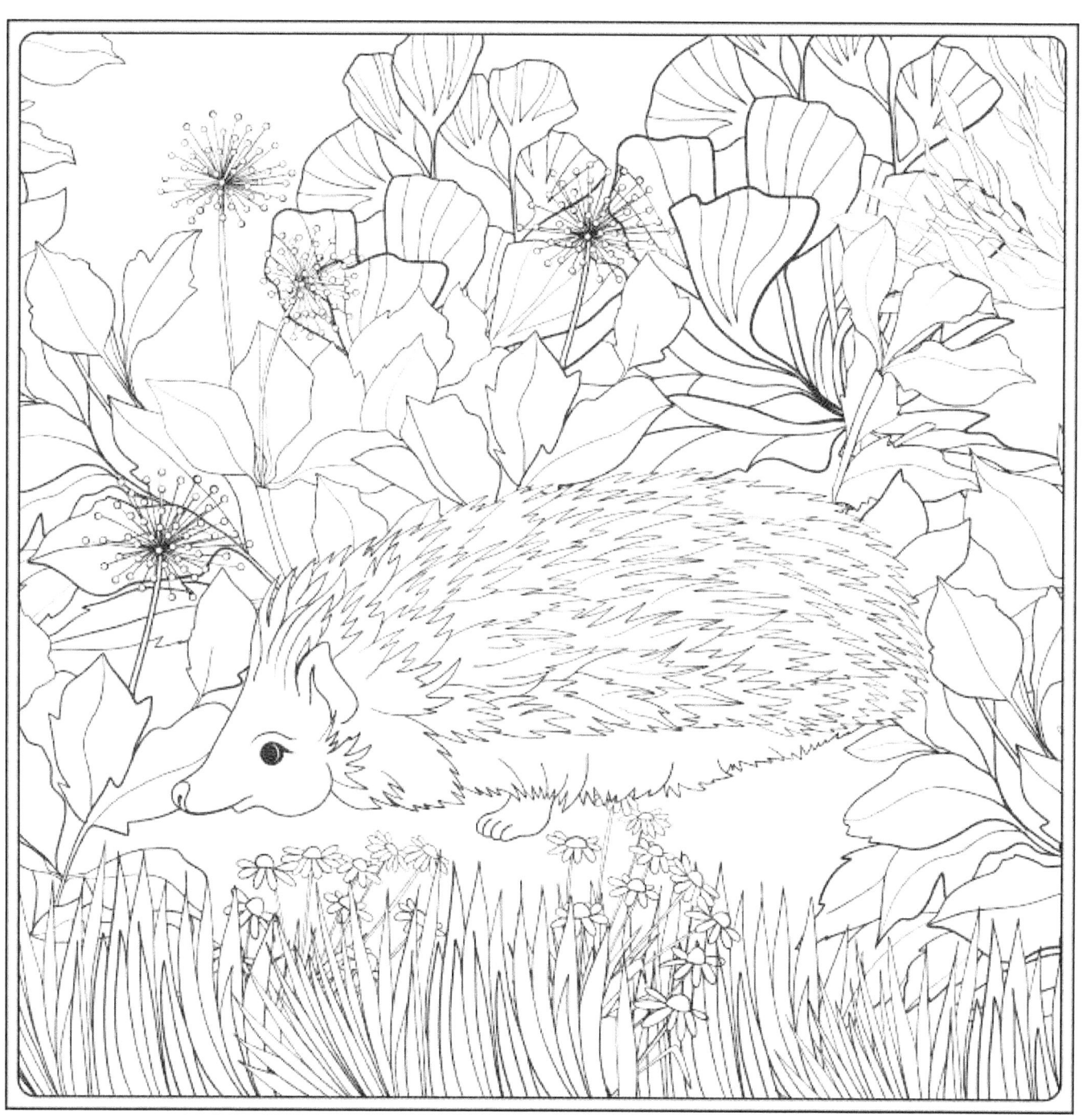

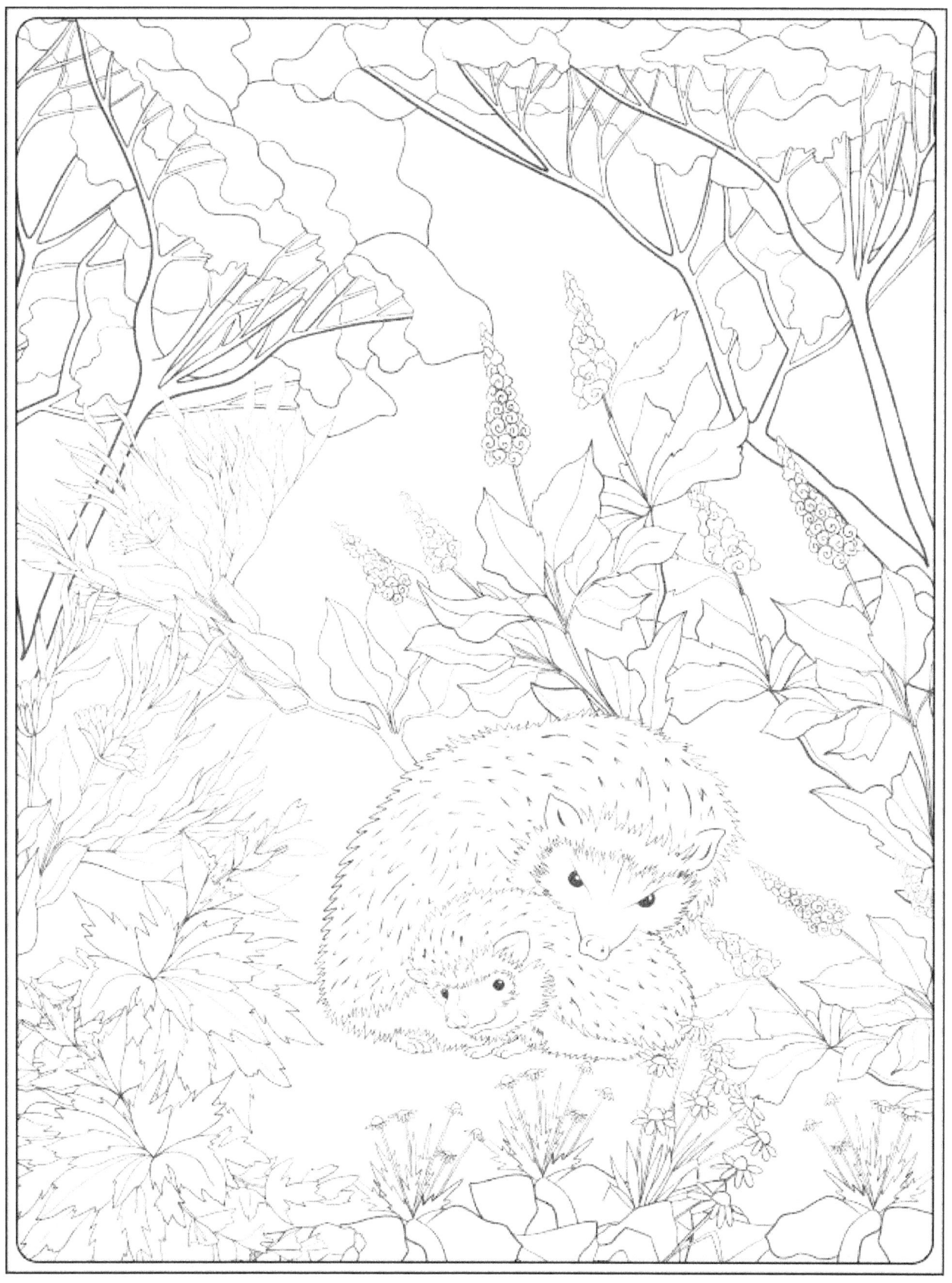

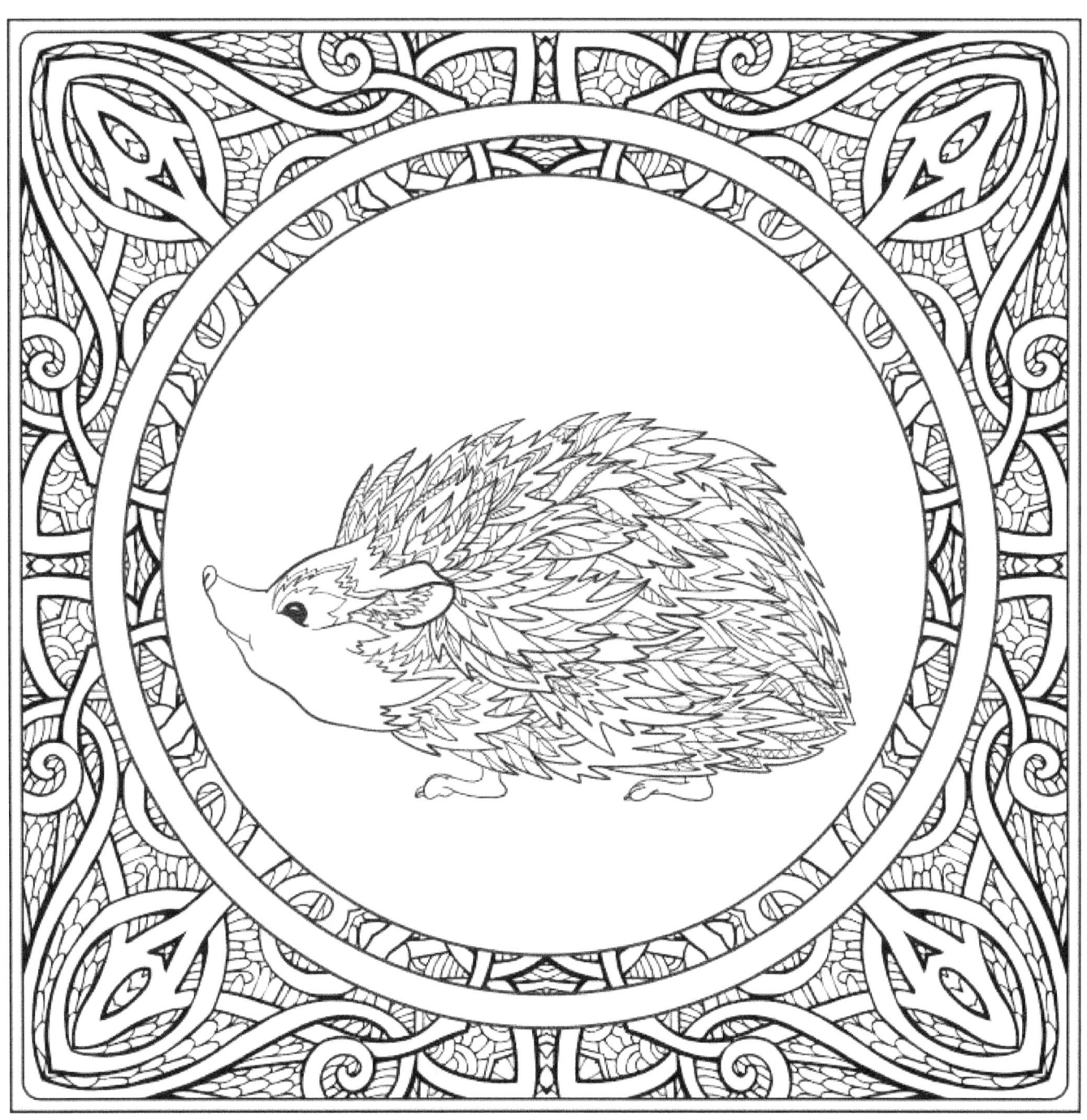

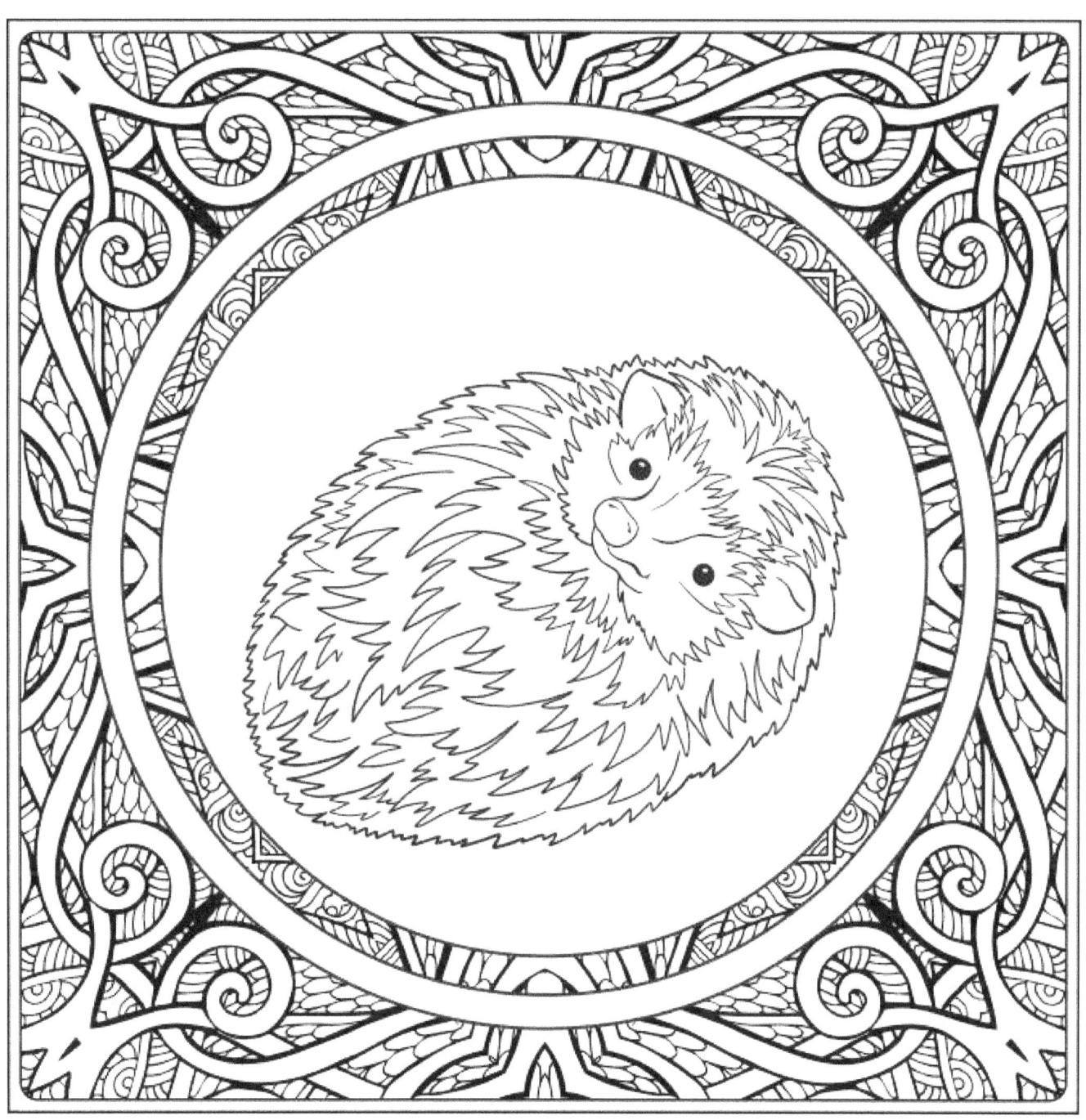

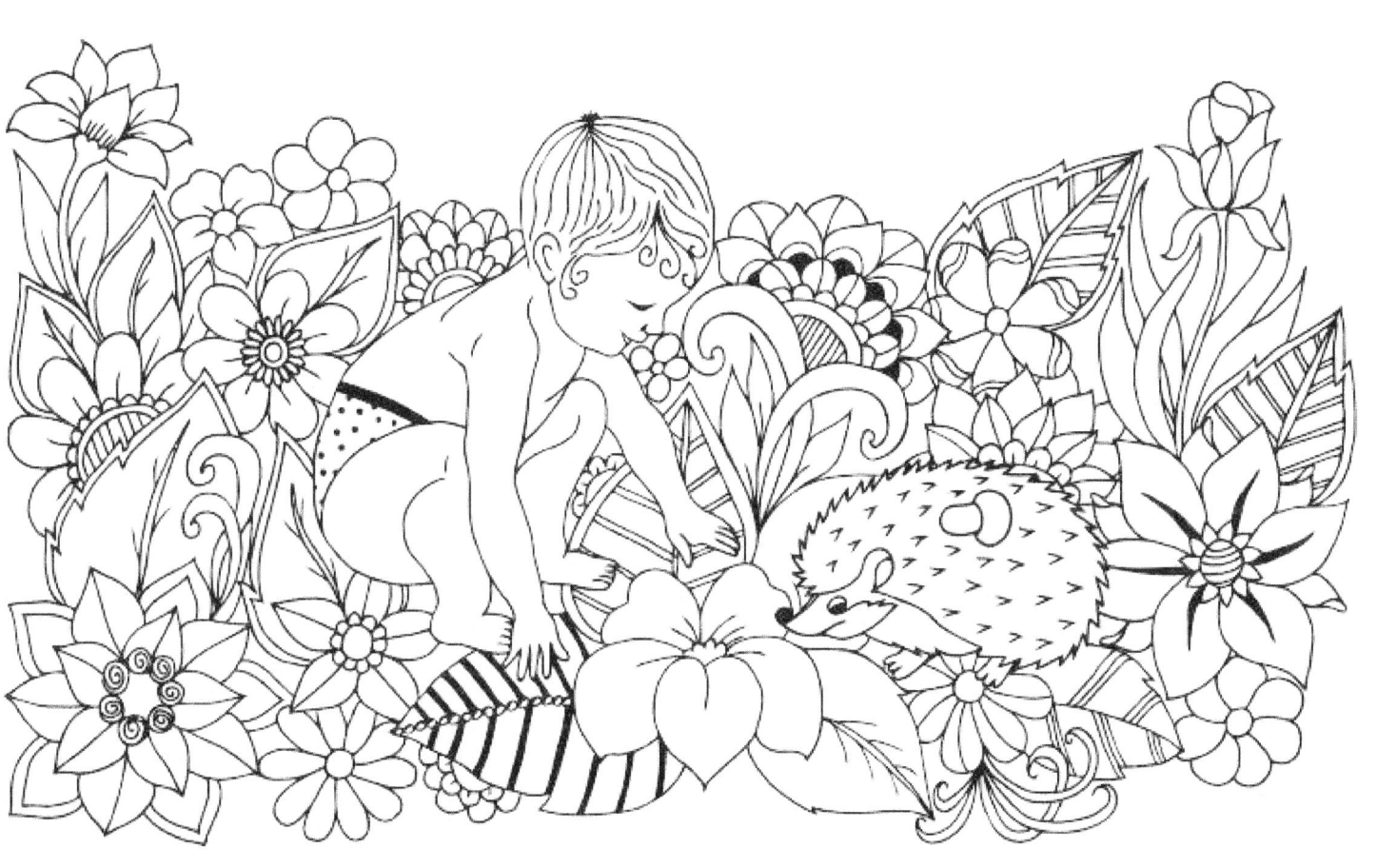

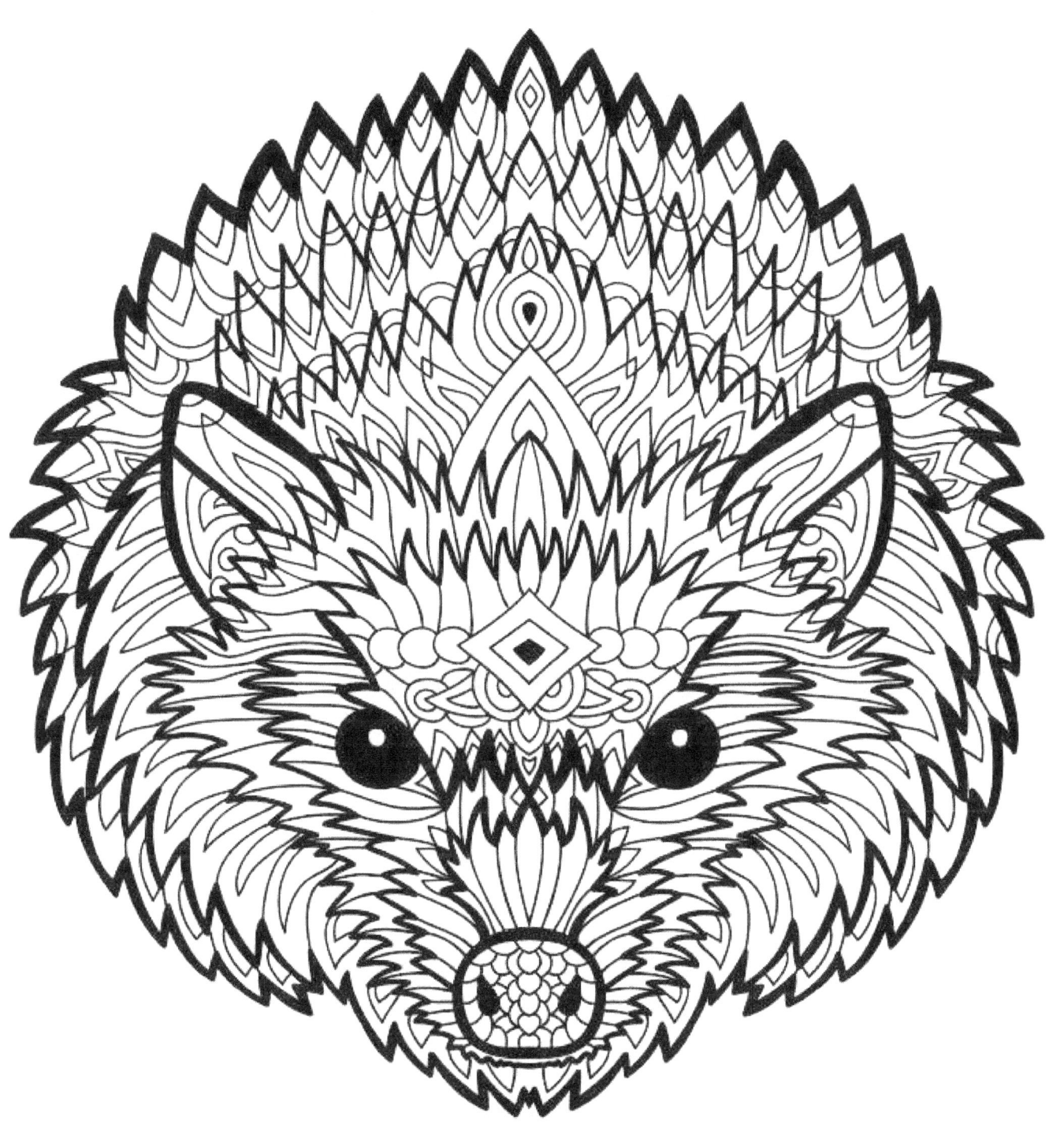

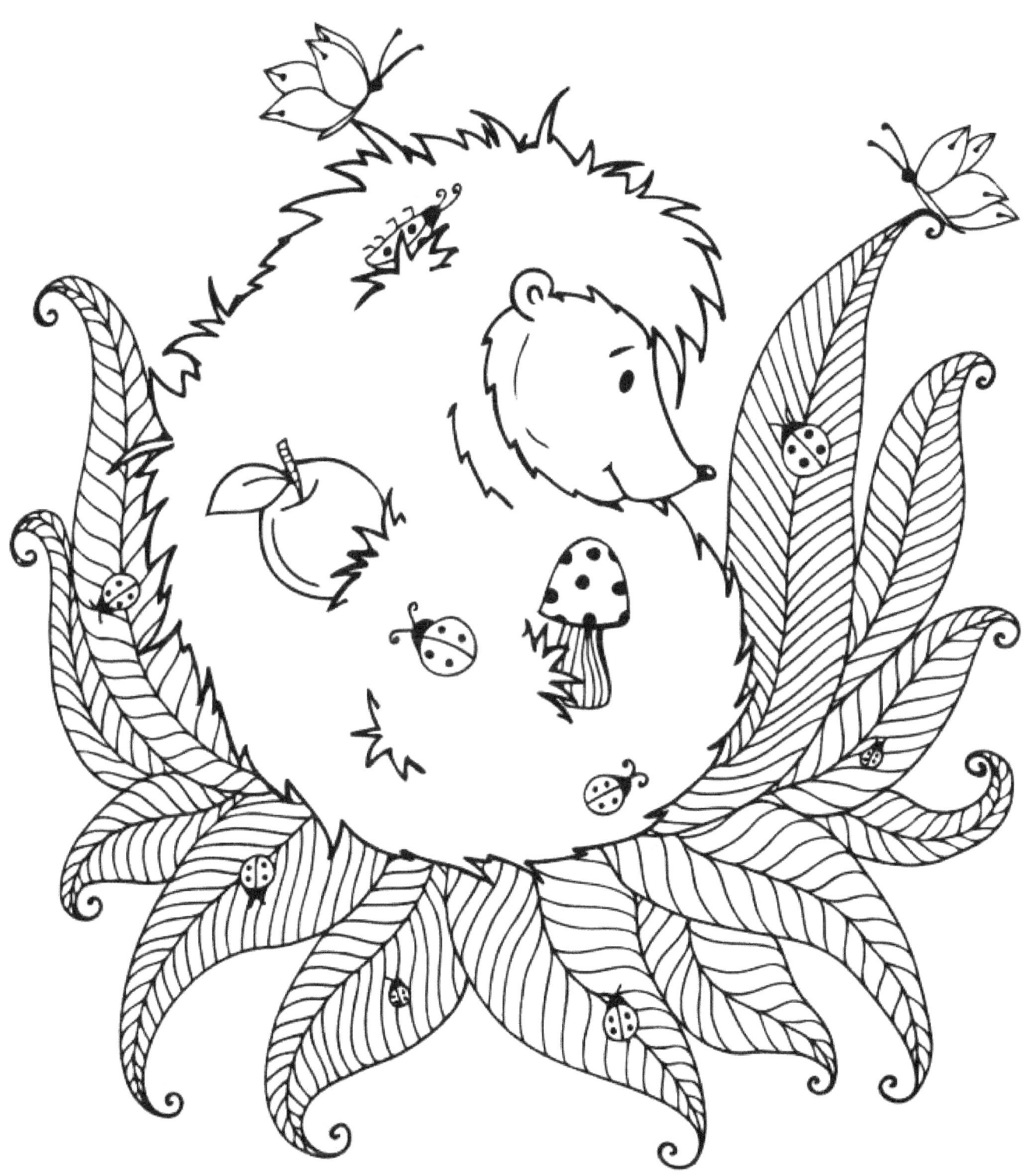

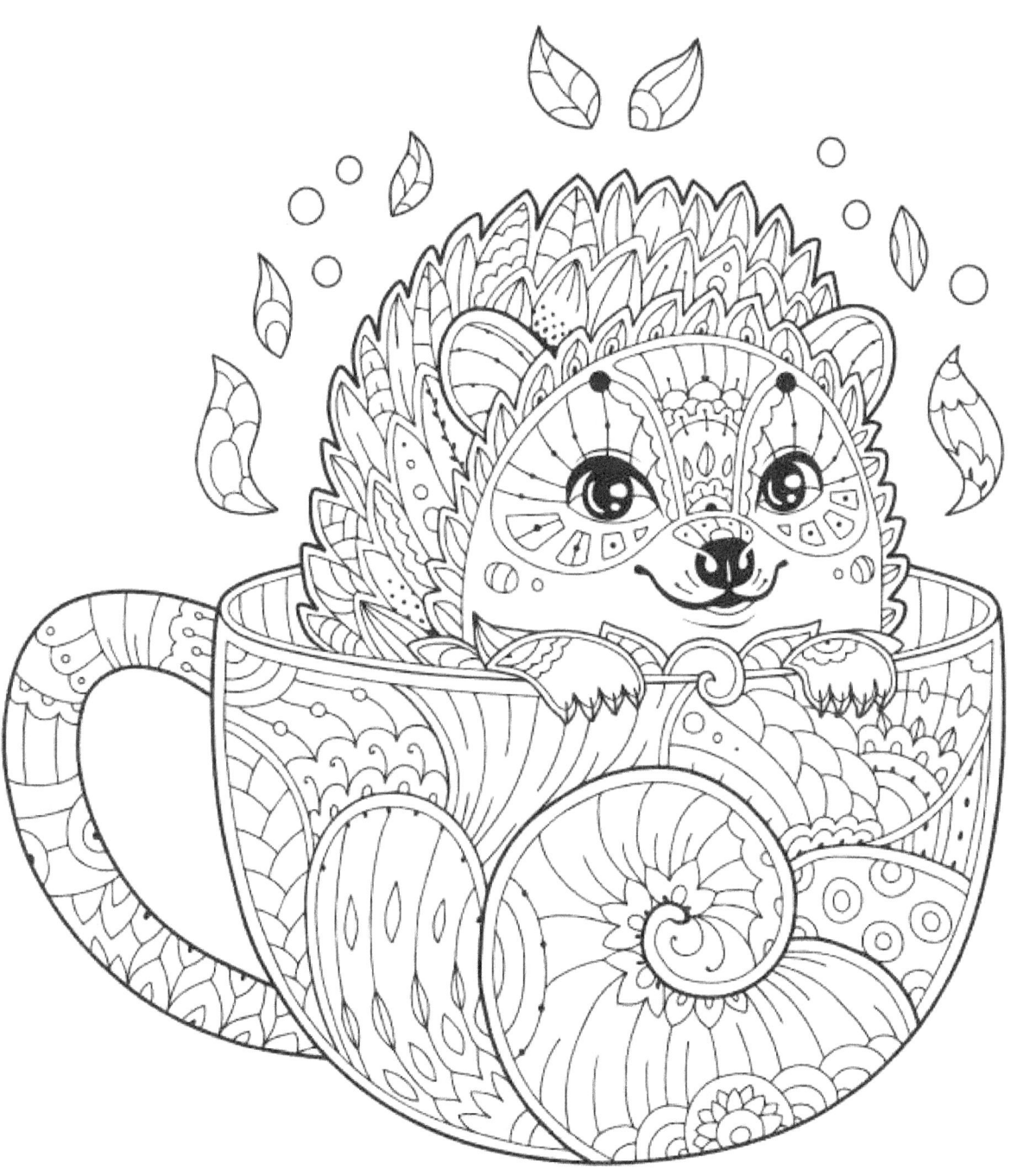

Surprise Bonus Turtle Coloring Illustrations for you to enjoy!

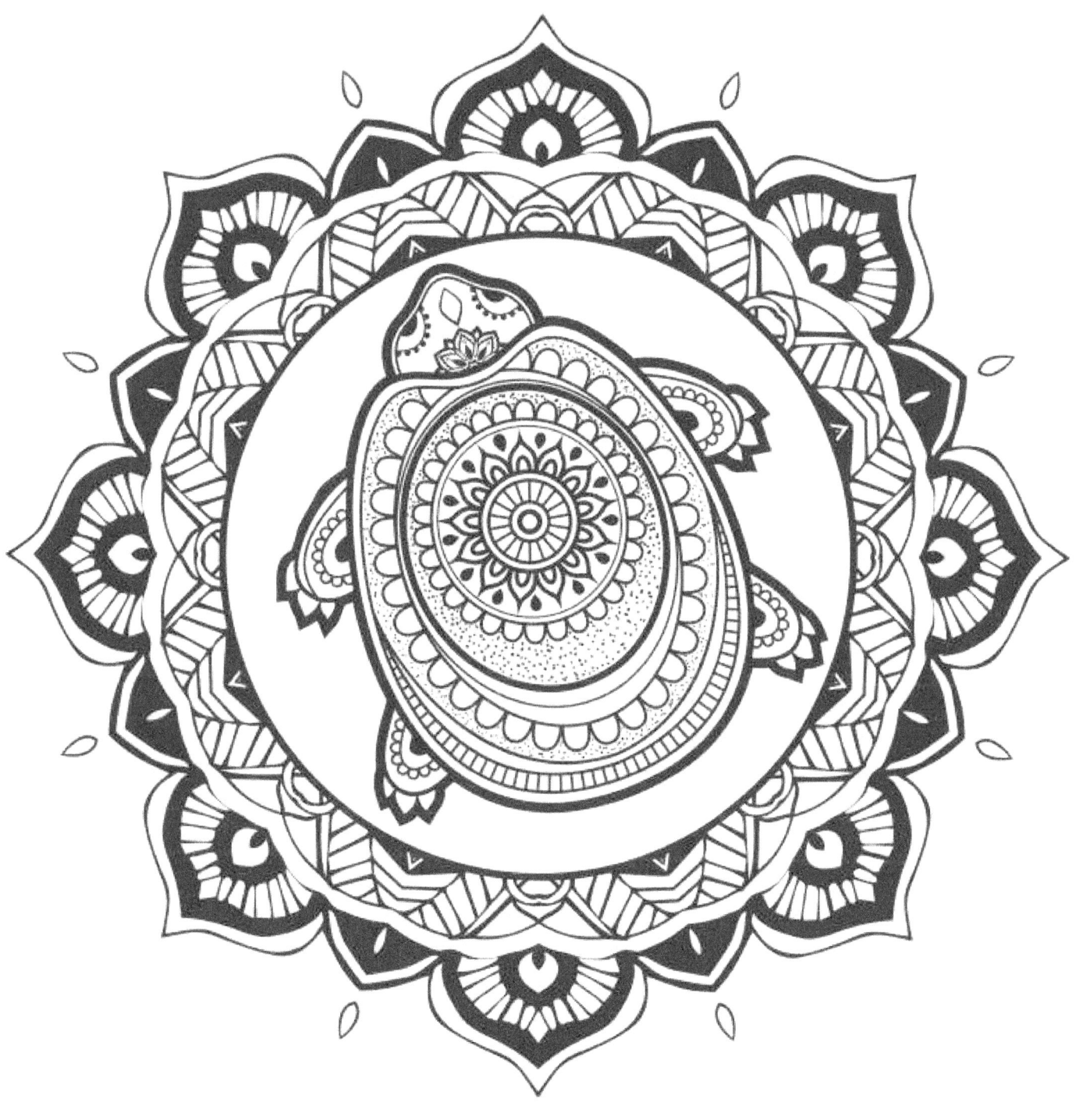

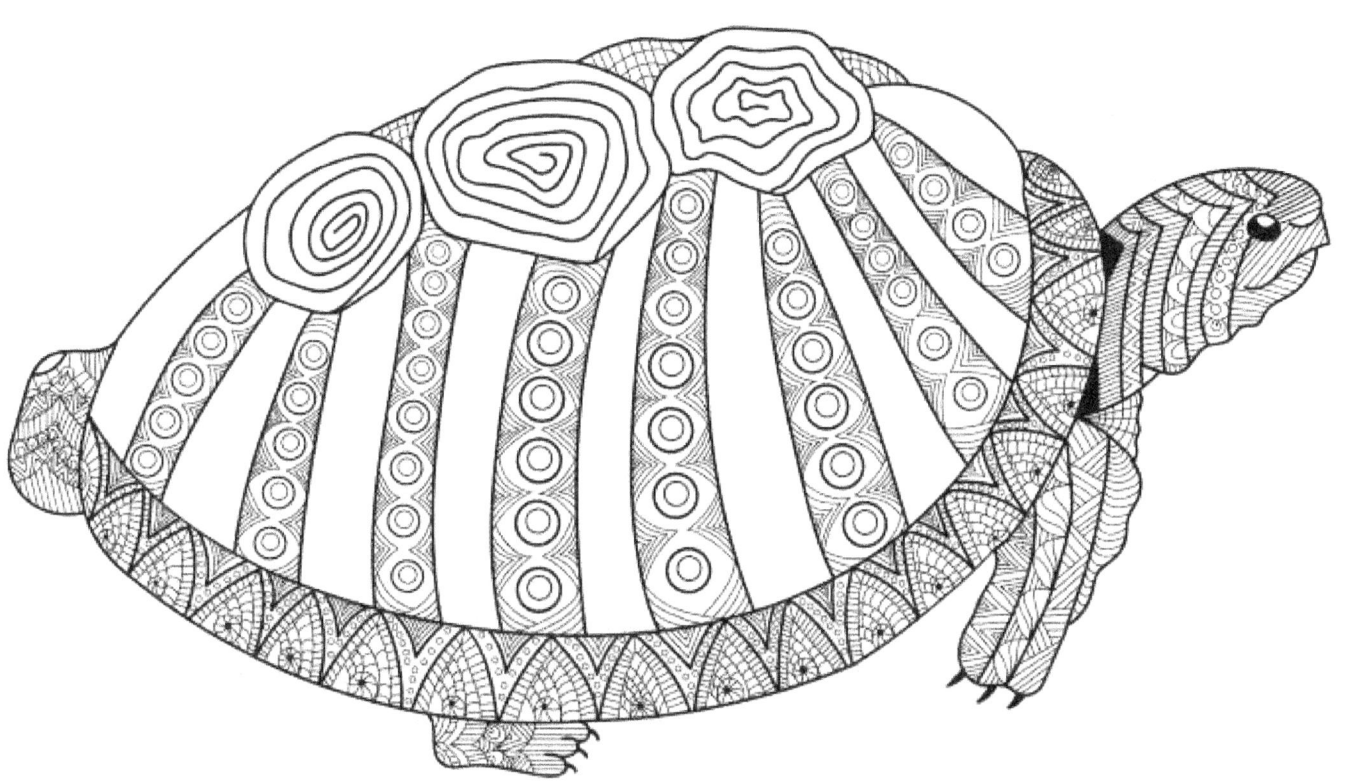

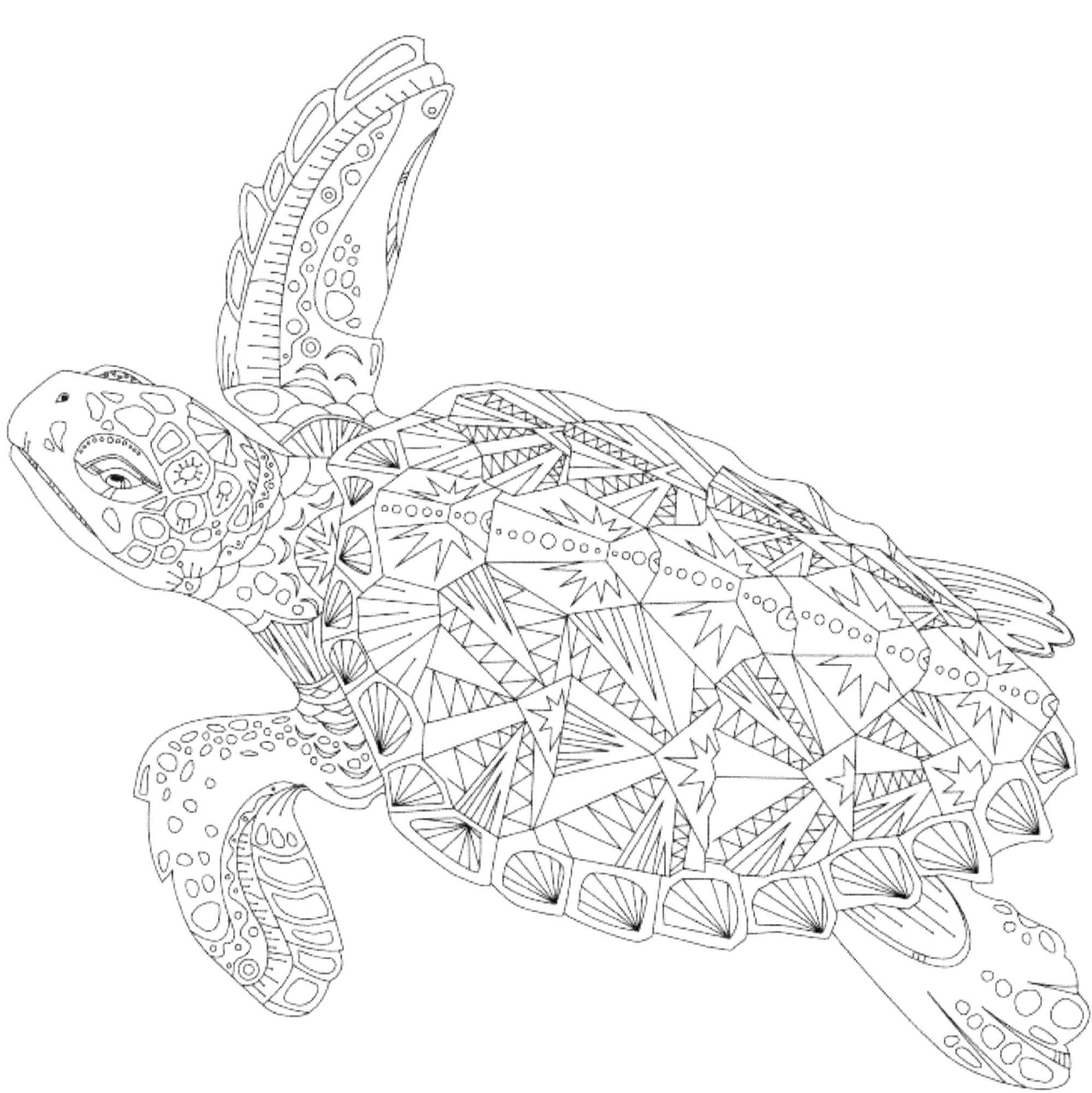

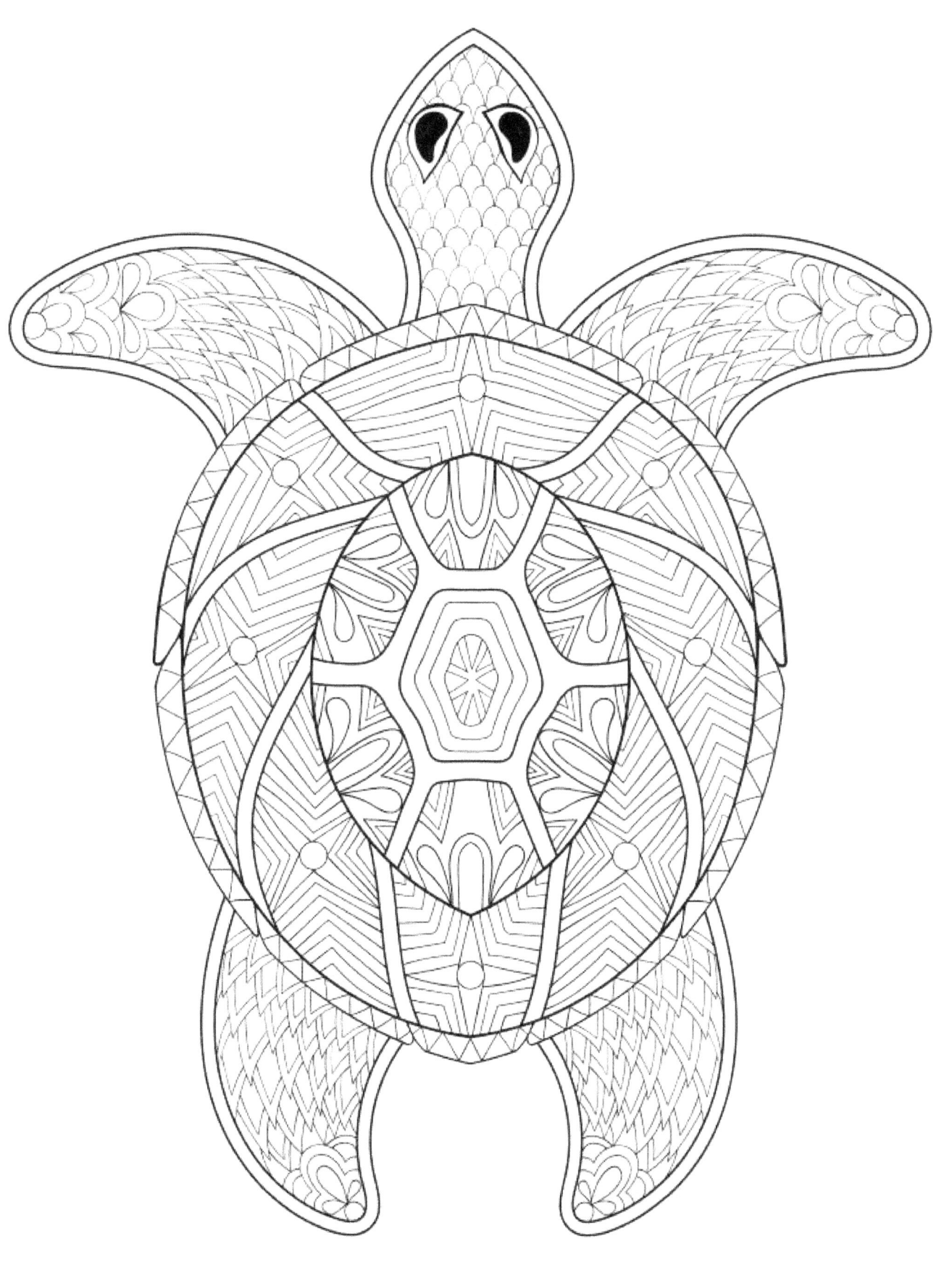

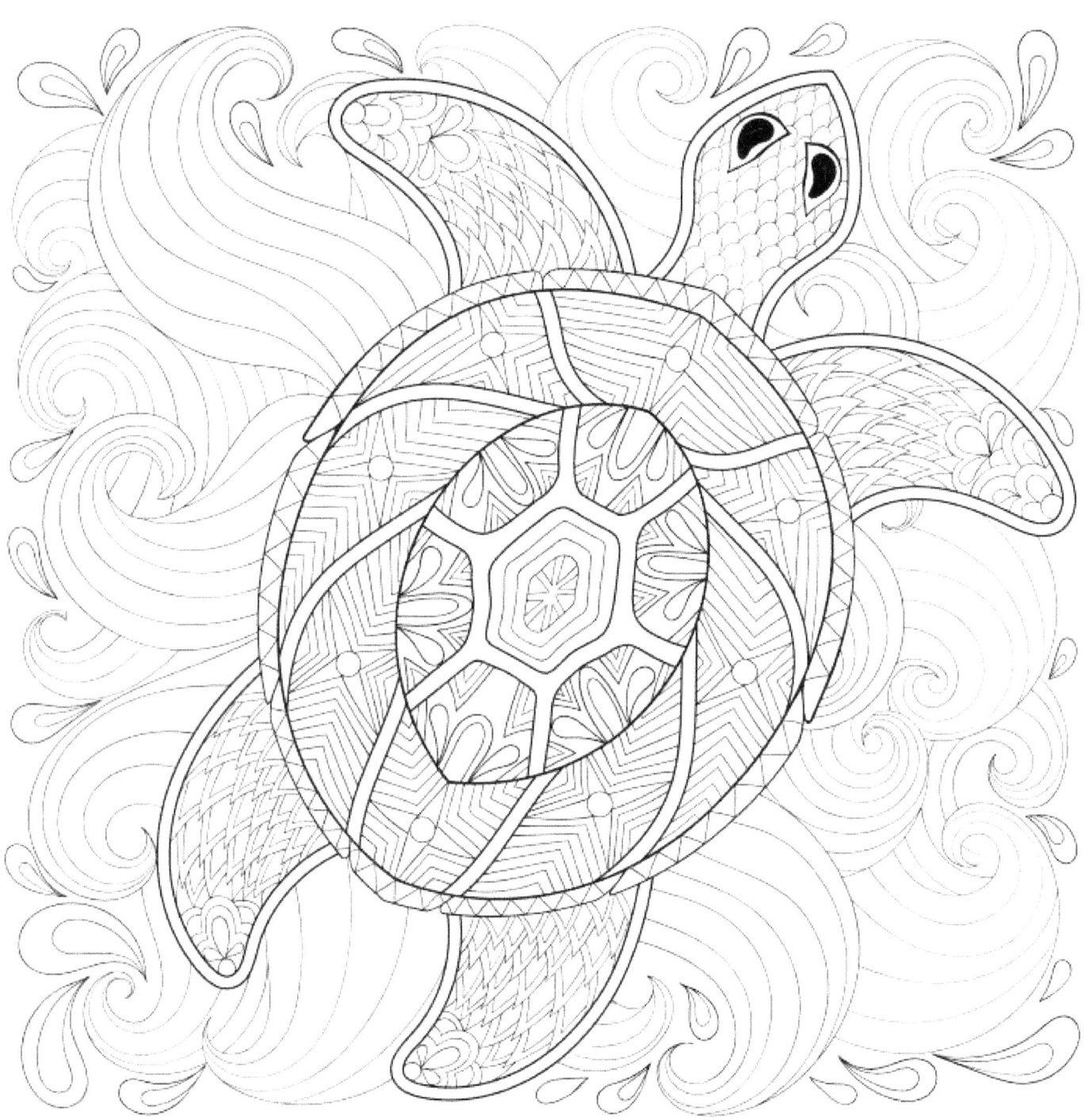

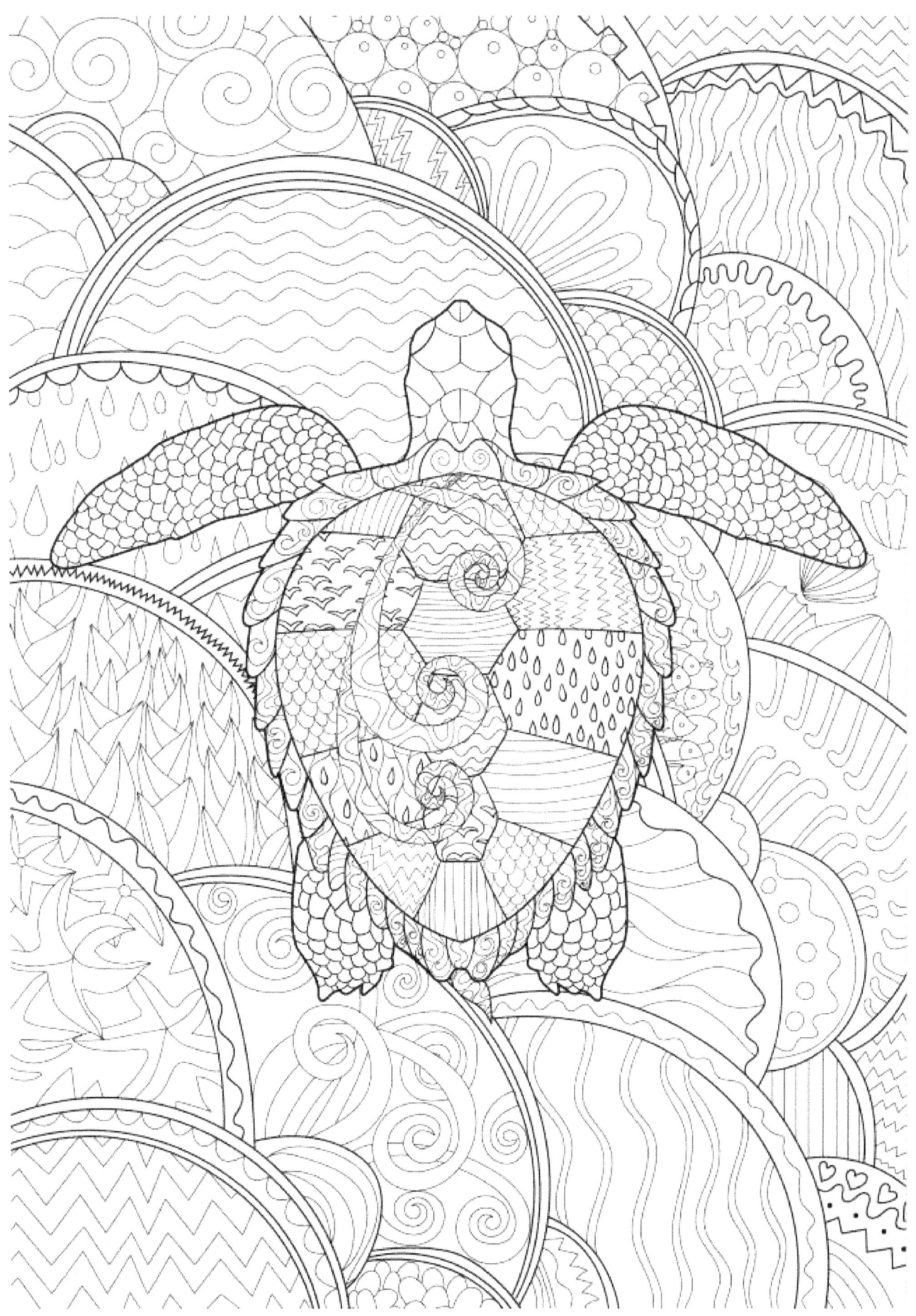

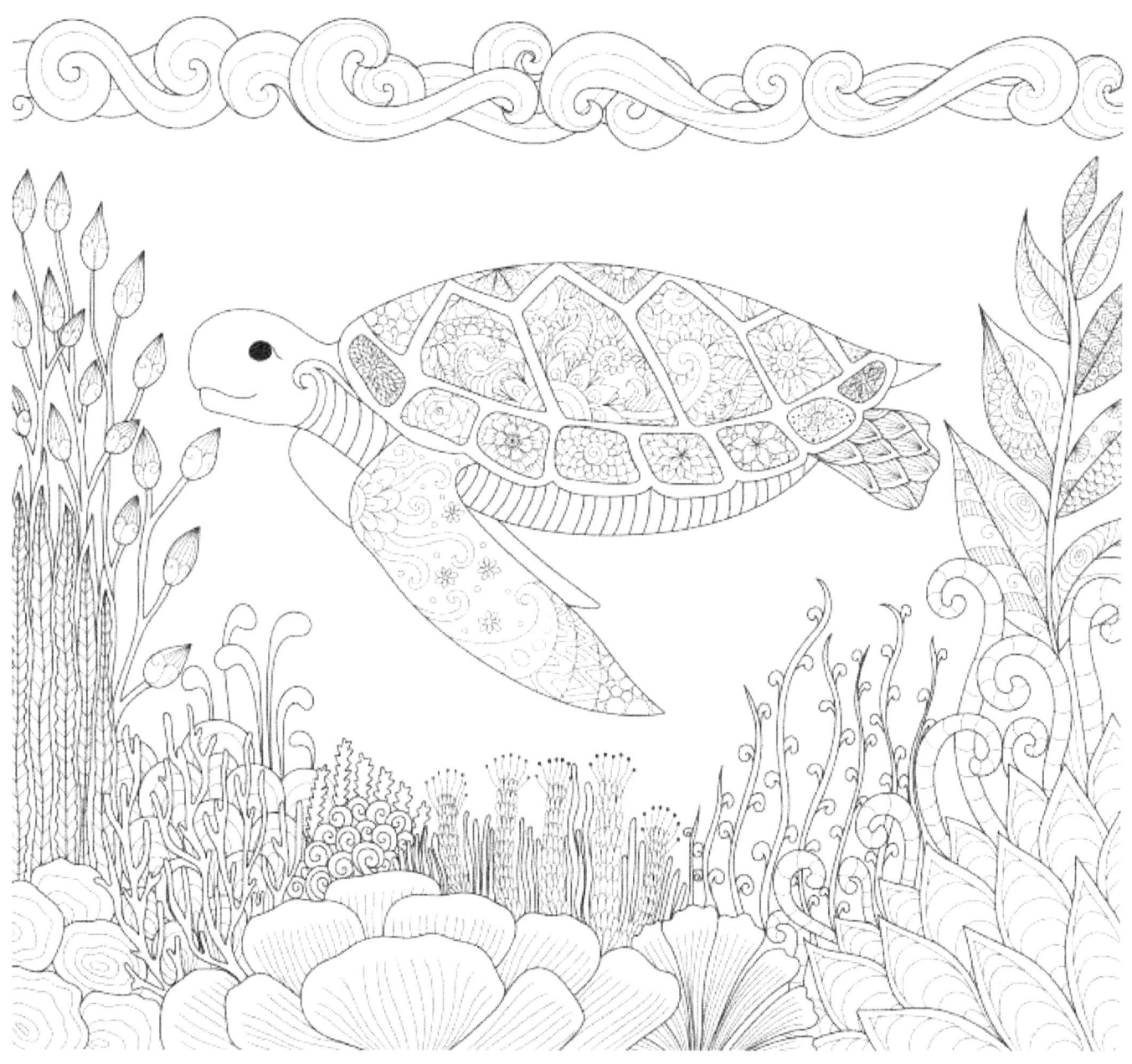

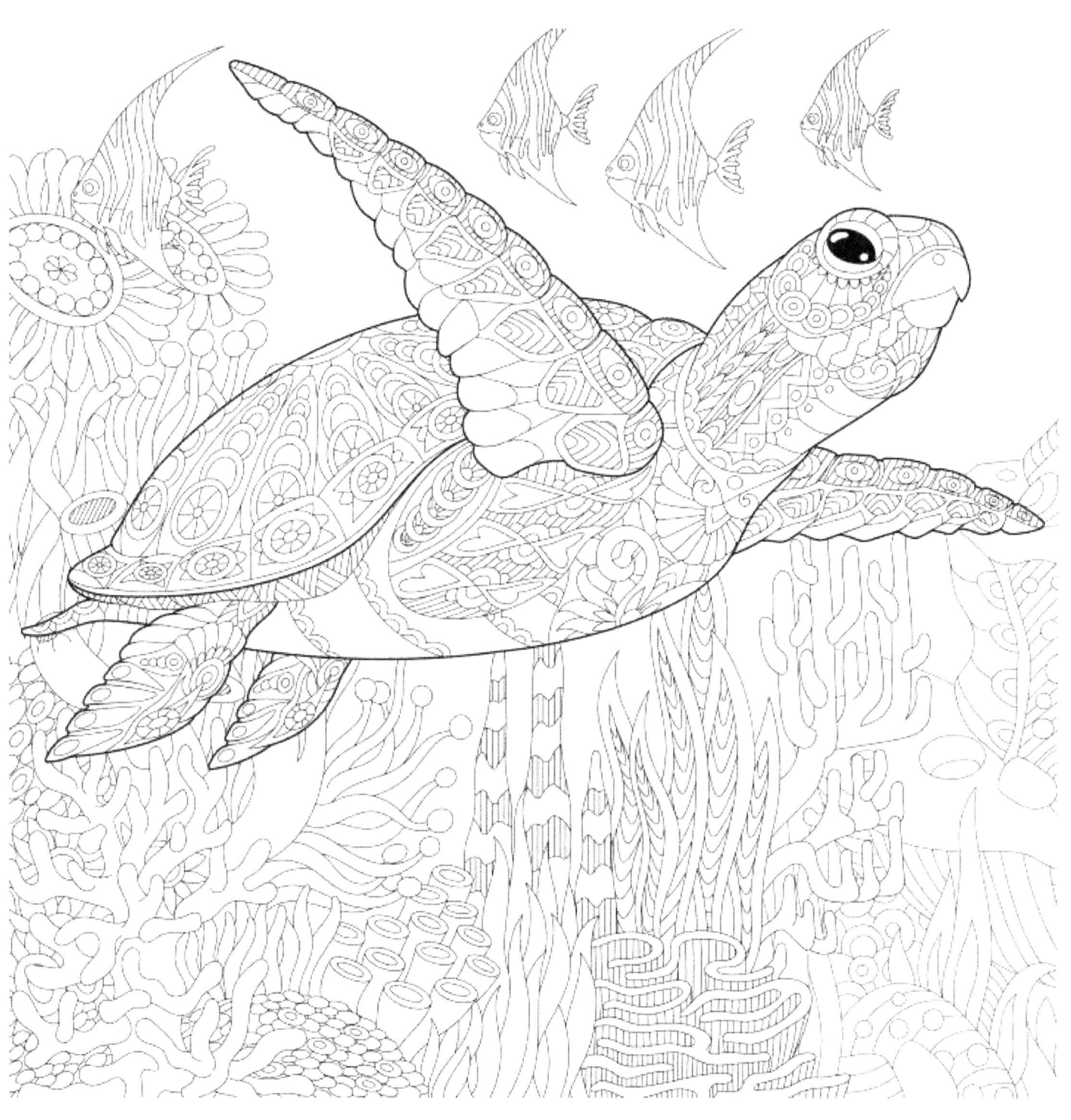

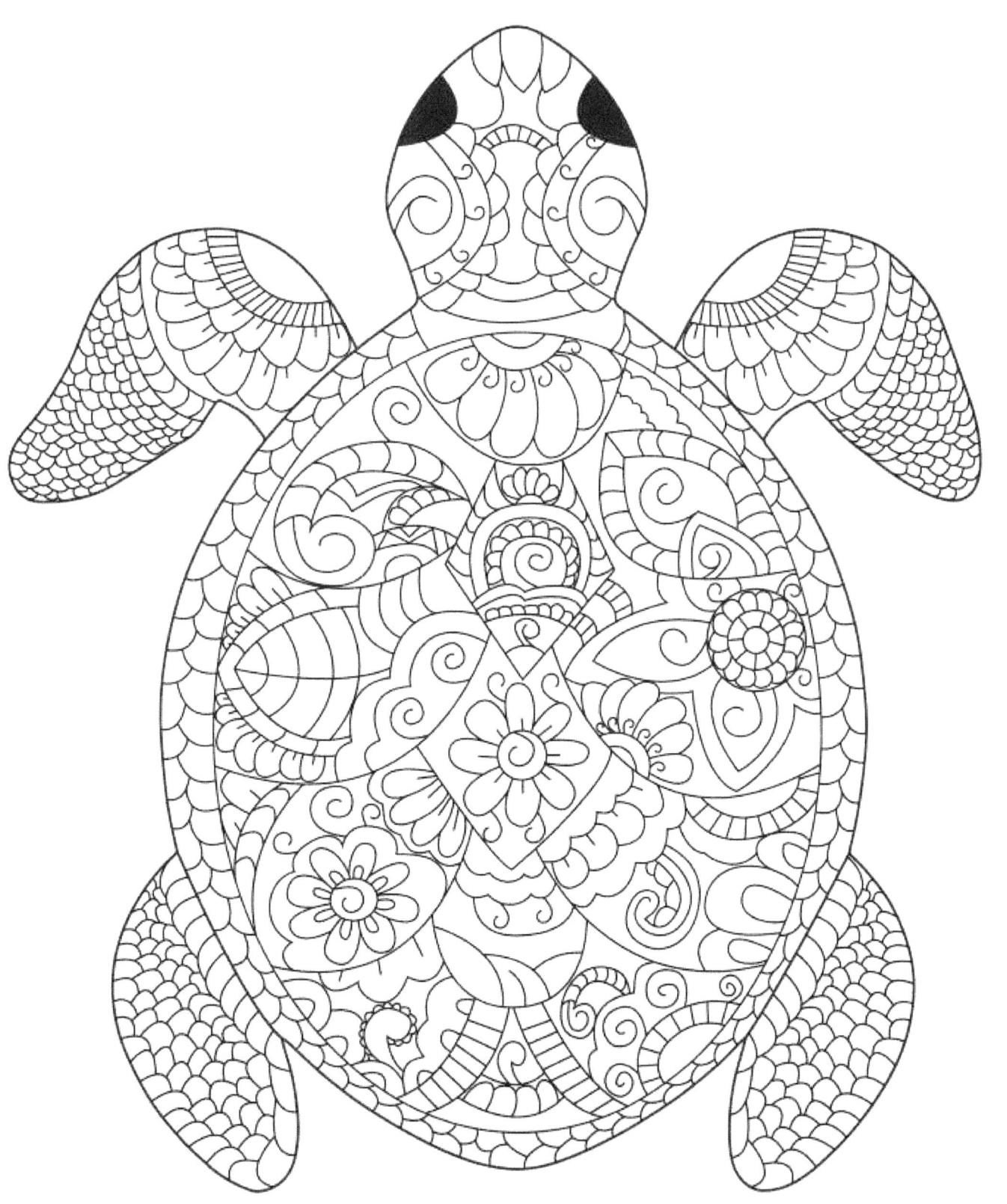

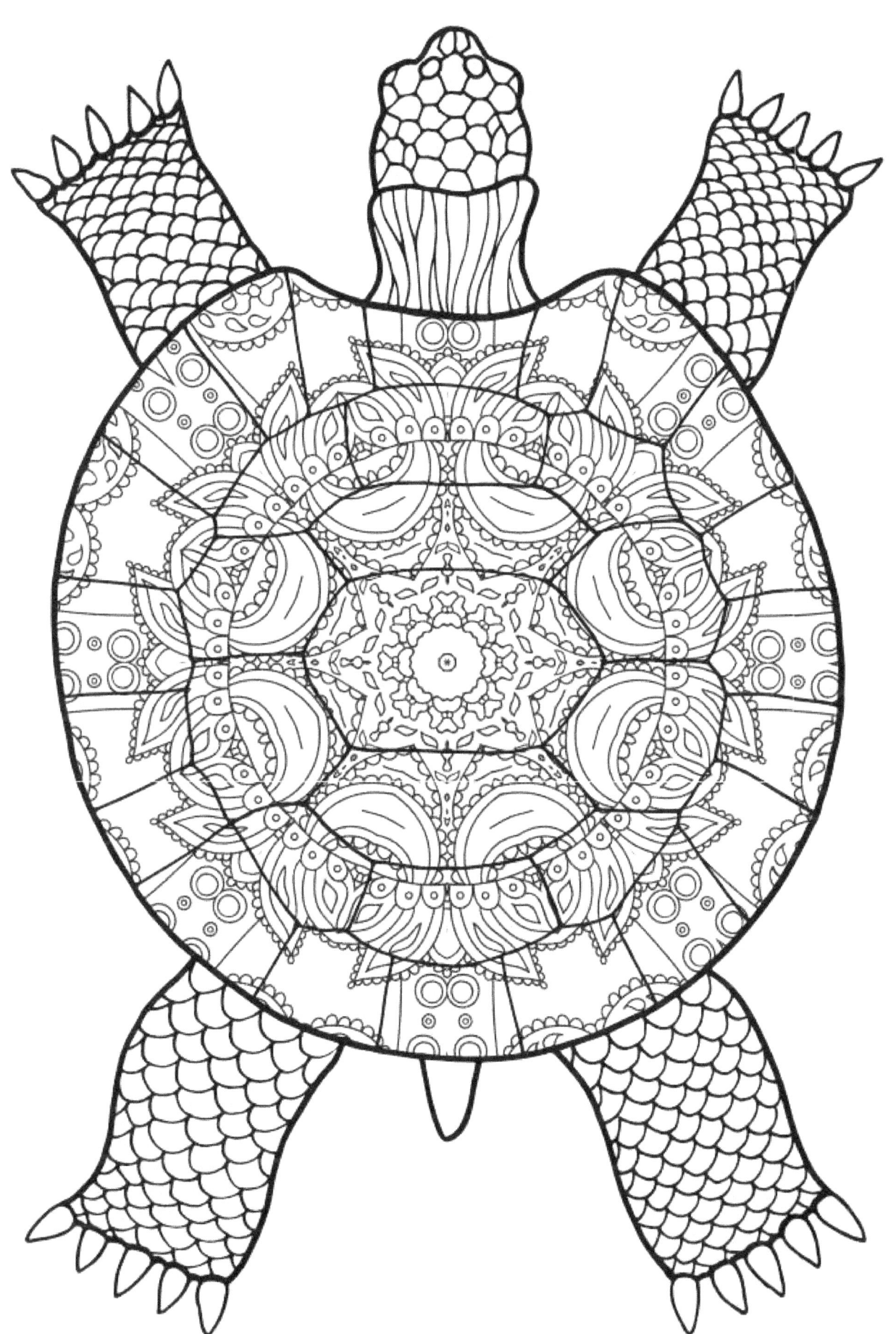

www.ingramcontent.com/pod-product-compliance
Lightning Source LLC
Chambersburg PA
CBHW081733170526
45167CB00009B/3805